Drawn to the Edge

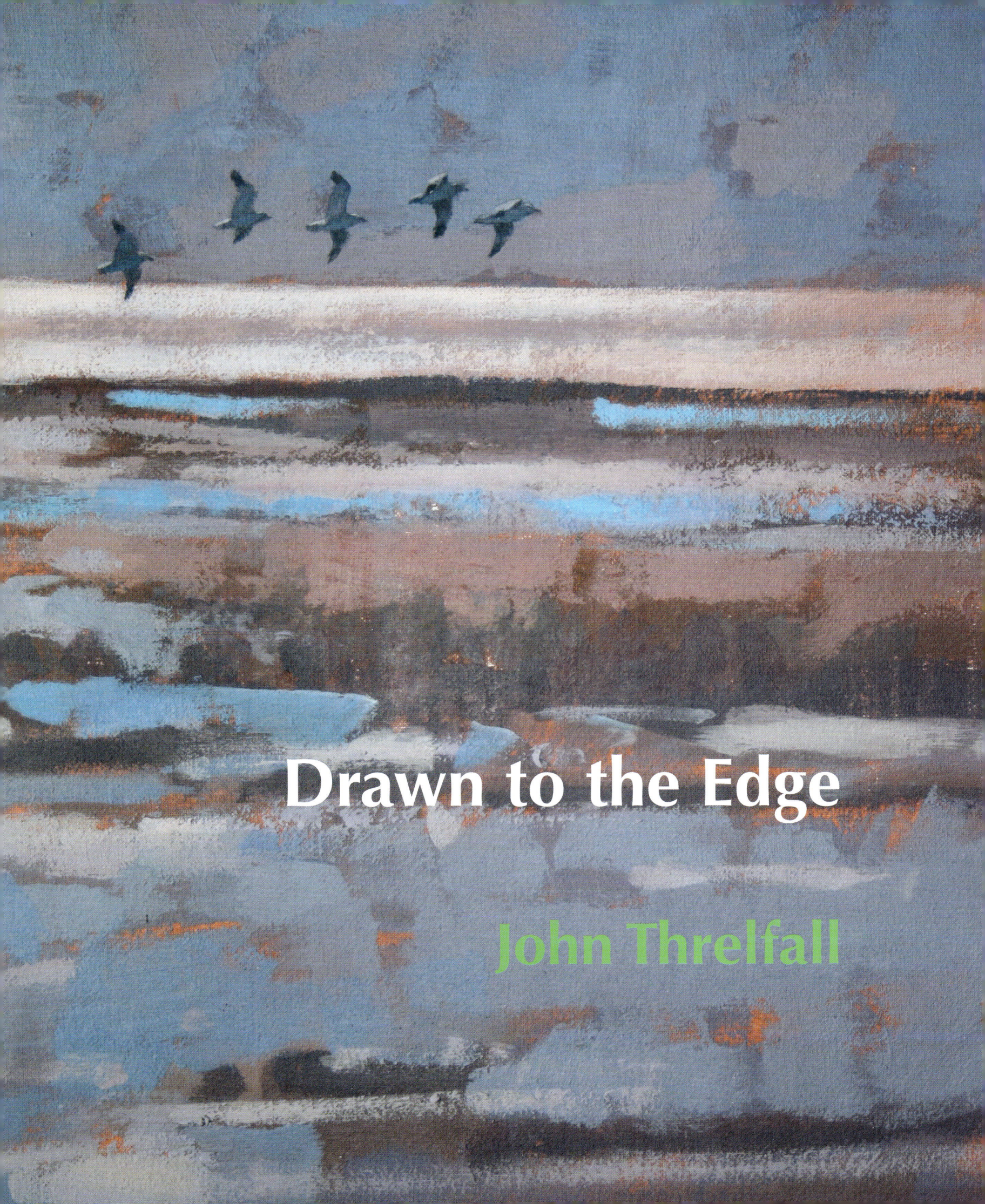

First published in 2013 by
Langford Press, 10 New Road, *Langtoft*
Peterborough PE6 9LE
www.langford-press.co.uk
Email sales@langford-press.co.uk

ISBN 978-1-904078-38-8

A CIP Record for this book is available
from the British Library

Text and images © 2013 John Threlfall

The rights of The Artist to be identified as the illustrators
of this work have been asserted in accordance with the
Copyright, Designs and Patents Act 1988.

John Threlfall has asserted his moral right to be
identified as author of this work under the Copyright,
Designs and Patents Act 1988.

Editorial consultant, Rob Hume
Origination design and typeset in Optima and Utopia by,
MRM Graphics Ltd, Winslow, Bucks
Printed in Spain

Front cover: *Towards White Nothe*, The Jurassic Coast, Dorset
Frontispiece: *Gull Wave*, Bamburgh, Northumberland

Contents

	Acknowledgements	VII
	Introduction	VIII
1	Seacliffs and sea stacks	1
2	Maritime heath and grassland	39
3	Rocky Shores	49
4	Shingle	79
5	Saline lagoons	91
6	Sandy beaches and dunes	101
7	Estuaries and saltmarsh	127
8	Sea lochs	157
9	Off shore islands	165
	Conclusion	188

FOR JUDY

Tollesbury,
Essex.
Watercolour

ACKNOWLEDGEMENTS

I wish to express my gratitude to those who have helped to turn this project into a reality, particularly Keith Allison at MRM Graphics and Stuart Fortune for the design of the book, to Rob Hume for reading through the text and making sense of it and especially to Ian Langford for making it all possible in the first place and entrusting me with this title.

Friends and family have always been there for support, even when they don't realise it, but specific thanks are due to Tim Wootton, John Cox, John Busby, David Mabbs, to Steve and Liz Harris at Birdscapes Gallery and to my wife Judy for all the love and laughter and just somehow coping with me all these years.

Arctic Tern, Foulney Island.
Watercolour

Introduction

South Luangwa National Park in Zambia may seem a strange place to begin a book on the coastal habitats and wildlife of the British Isles, but please stay with me for a moment.

This was October 2008, my long awaited first visit to Africa, and I was overwhelmed by the experience. It had a huge impact on me. To encounter elephants, lions and buffaloes from the relative safety of the back of a jeep is one thing; to come face to face with them on foot was entirely different. This untameable wildness, with its pulsing soundscape, was raw, visceral and exciting.

There was a keen edged drama throughout much of the time, usually involving the aforementioned mega fauna plus crocodiles. Lions didn't so much as look at you as through you. You knew your place. Lessons in humility are always beneficial! A heightened sense of awareness became a natural state, awe and astonishment were prevalent, a state of alert preferable and you felt very much alive. I wasn't ready to come home.

Britain seemed tame, bland, colourless and dull in comparison. Our natural environment has been sanitised, neutered, repressed, all wild threats to our safety and well-being and livelihoods ruthlessly exterminated. Consequently we have become desensitised, estranged from nature, indifferent, numb, dehumanised. Strong words, but these were my thoughts at the time.

Three weeks later, I was on the North Norfolk coast, staying at Salthouse and determined to be out and about from early dawn to make the most of the brief winter's day. Cattle slowly graze their way through the remnant grass-dew mist, an enthusiasm of starlings probing possibilities, a scattering of lapwings use an altogether more studious approach. As I make my way towards the shingle bank, shrill, clamorous redshanks heckle me, affronted by the temerity of my presence. A mid distant gathering of greylag geese takes to the sharpening air adding more sheaves of sound. The primitive croak of a little egret precedes its short, shuttlecock-light flight into the next drainage ditch. Goldfinches feed nervously on seed heavy plants and three brisk snow buntings, glimpsed as they disappear round a corner. Brent geese, holding the line of the beach, break overhead and my heart really leaps at the sight of a short-eared owl, starting low towards me across the marsh and, at piercing stare distance, easing aloofly away, trailing my gaze in its wake. I love the aloofness of owls!

At long last, as if from a disturbed sleep, I had woken. I had woken to the wildness of this morning, to that fervent force of life that grabs you and shakes some sense into you, that slices clean through your fawning insensitivities, peeling away churlishly crafted ideals, to reveal your own true, wild core and penetrate to the truth of the matter. We are nature, we are not separate from nature nor above it, and my awakening was to that fact, to that reconnection. I felt fully alive again.

A visit to our coast can do this to you, time and time again. It can open you up. Just staring out to sea, out onto the wide levels: how contemplative, calming, relaxing and awe inspiring it is. It is safe to say that it has stirred emotions in man ever since there have been eyes and a conscience there to dwell upon the view. More than ever, perhaps, it is the appeal of a simple horizoned landscape in increasingly cluttered lives. Maybe it is just that tangy sea fresh air that compels you to breathe more deeply, more slowly, or the invocation of sun creamed childhood holidays on the beach.

Where the sea and land meet is still so often where we play and rest, where our distant hunter-gatherer ancestry resurfaces as we explore rock pools, or search for beautiful shells and pebbles to collect, or find sea sculpted driftwood forms, or the magic and mystery of fossils. What a thrill it is to find your own ammonite or belemnite. There is always a bit of the beachcomber in all of us! The work surfaces for my first studio were constructed from crates and palettes washed up on the beach.

Maybe it is just the "blowing the cobwebs away" sensation that only a walk along wind tormented cliff tops can give you; the wind in your hair, the glow on your face, the sound of the waves below, a feeling of remoteness, of wildness.

Combine that with a visit to a breeding seabird colony in spring or early summer and prepare to be overwhelmed by a planetary phenomenon, a life force of nature. The sheer raucousness of it all, the unceasing, incessant, cacophonous, beautiful din of it all, the slightly nauseous, pungent, throat choking smell of it all, the stirring, swirling, bemusing movement of it all, the wind wild ruggedness, the ravishing spectacle. Thrift and sea campion spilling colour over the edge, fulmars and kittiwakes hanging buoyantly on the updraughts, delightedly revelling in the lift, the wing whirring blurring flight of razorbills, the streamline smooth sculptural forms of guillemots, the radiantly bright white angularity of gannets, the charming, beguiling innocence of puffins, the aerial perfection of peregrines. We are in a world of superlatives here.

Eight million seabirds come to the UK each year to breed. The islands and cliffs around our coast offer perfect nesting sites and the surrounding seas provide rich feeding grounds. As the cold sea currents of the Arctic move south to meet the warm currents of the Gulf Stream there is a mixing and upwelling of nutrients, food for plankton; and plankton are in turn food for fish.

This coming together of earth and ocean is an exhilarating, life enhancing place and as an island nation with a coastline in excess of 7,500 miles, we have more than enough opportunities to stand and stare. To paraphrase Edward Abbey, "here is the power of the unexpected to startle the senses and surprise the mind out of its ruts of habit, to compel us into a reawakened awareness of the wonderful, that which is full of wonder."

It has been my pleasure to explore our coastline and its exciting diversity of habitats and wildlife. It is not just the length of that coastline but the sheer number of different habitats that are way beyond the scope of this one book, so I have been necessarily selective. I have had to concentrate on the major habitats and on a few representative locations.

The weather has been testing at times. I have been down to a tee shirt before winter was out and worn multiple layers, scarf, hat and gloves in midsummer, waterproofs and a sheltering umbrella always at the ready. The wind demands that everything be clipped onto the drawing board and I have left a bulldog clip trail around the UK coast, such are the number that have mysteriously gone missing!

Apart from a brief explanation of the habitats at the start of each chapter, the text that accompanies the paintings is in the form of "coast-it" notes. These are jottings, ramblings and reflections, findings, observations and bits of information gleaned along the way.

There are some regrets; no shearwaters or petrels or rock doves or hoodie craws and I apologise for these and many other omissions. The regrets are few, however, compared to the profusion of highlights along this journey. The next time that I return from some exotic overseas visit, I will know exactly what the remedy is!

Puffins,
Castle O'Burrian,
Westray
Watercolour

Sea Cliffs and Stacks

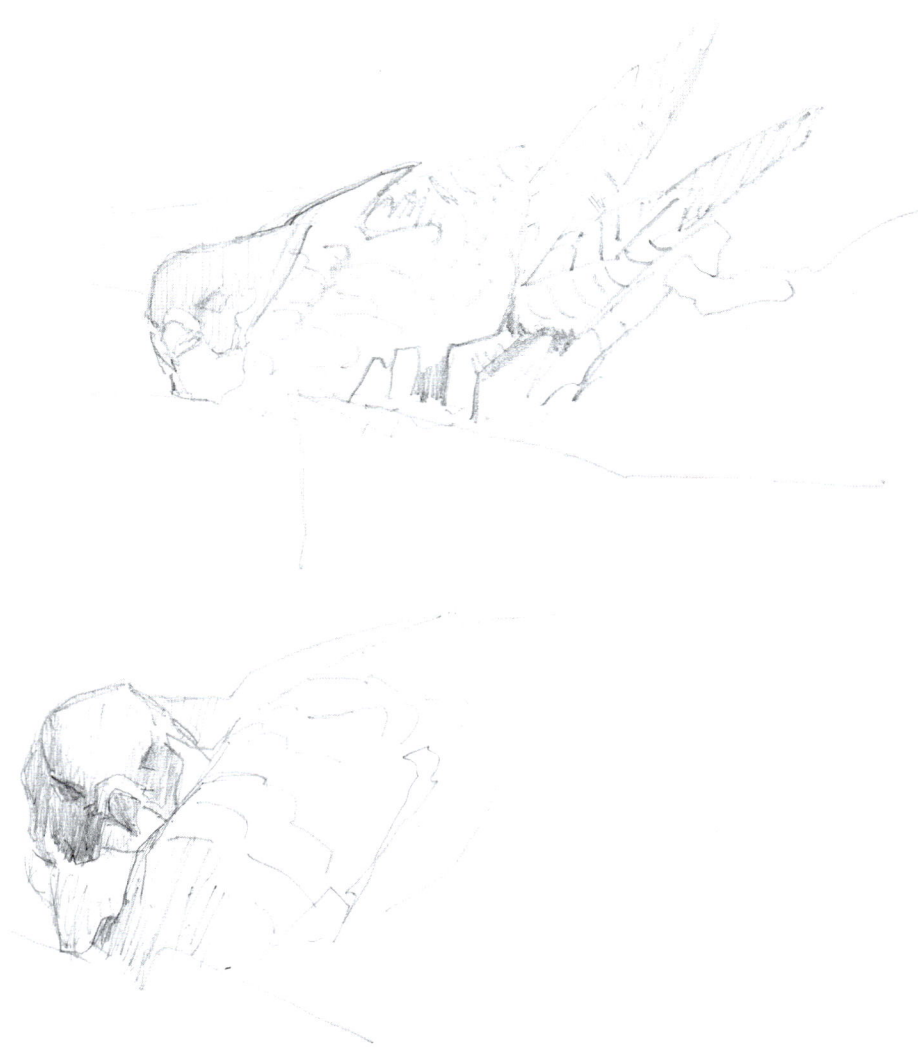

Here is where the land reveals its core, where rambling moors and grasslands end abruptly in sliced, giddy verticals. Much of the "excitement" of our landscape is in this contrast. To walk towards this edge always has a feel of the unexpected, one of startling surprise, the shock of the real, an awakening.

From April to August these teeming high rise tenements gift us an internationally acknowledged spectacle. The majority of these seabirds

Kittiwake Nest
The crumbling walls of boulder red sandstone blocks are
all that remain of the old castle in Dunbar harbour
Ancient handmade ledges   to kittiwake specifications

Dunbar, East Lothian.
Oil

spend their lives on the open ocean but they do have to come to land to nest and to raise their young. The inaccessibility of high cliff faces and sea stacks provides protection from disturbance and land predators.

Four members of the auk family may be found. The disarming charm of puffins delights us all and since they tend to nest in burrows in the soft turf atop a sea stack, or in rocky nooks towards the top of mainland cliffs, close views can be enjoyed. By contrast, black guillemots, or tysties, tend to nest towards the base of cliffs in caves or crevices. Guillemots favour narrow ledges on the face itself and their uniquely conical shaped eggs are designed to spin on the spot if moved, rather than rolling over the edge, as well as being easier to incubate. The eggs of the razorbill are of a more conventional shape so they, too, seek out hollows and crevices in which to breed.

The attractive kittiwakes are the most numerous gull species on cliff sites, having the dexterity to construct a nest on ledges too narrow for even guillemots. Fulmars, like miniature albatrosses, stiff winged in flight, nest in hollows towards the cliff top.

Fulmars
Balcary Heughs,
Dumfries and Galloway.
Watercolour

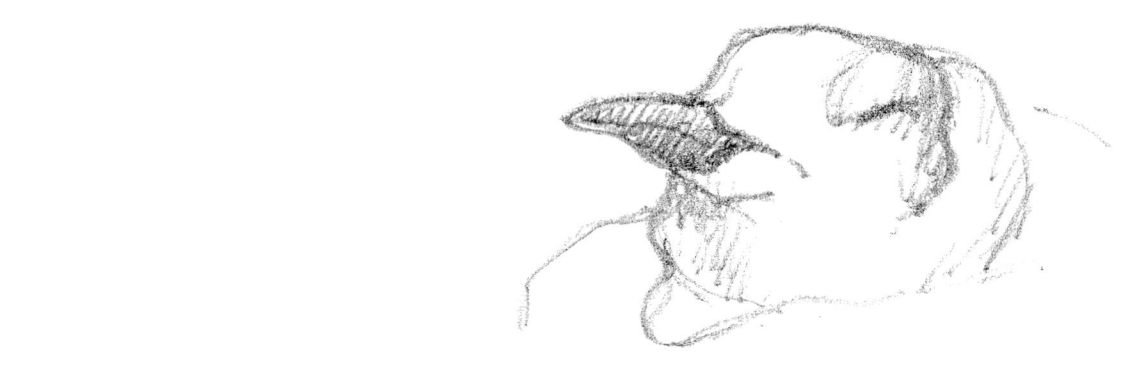

Guillemots
Brough of Birsay,
Orkney.
Pencil

4 SEA CLIFFS AND STACKS

Gannets, the UK's biggest seabirds with a wingspan of two metres, occur at only two mainland sites, Bempton Cliffs in East Yorkshire and at Troup Head in Aberdeenshire. The numbers at Bempton have increased exponentially in recent years, from 30 pairs in 1970 to 6,000 pairs today. They are beautiful birds with a remarkable lifestyle. As you stand on a cliff top, these impressive creatures going by at eye level are something to behold.

The glossy dark green coloured shags construct large nests of seaweed and vegetation and so require wider ledges or larger crevices and gullies. They may nest singly or in larger colonies. Shags (and their close cousins the cormorants) are less oceanic than the other seabirds, having feathers that are less water repellent than other species. Consequently they have to leave the water after each feeding foray to preen and hang their wings out to dry, and so feed close to land.

Mainland cliff faces are home to birds other than seabirds. Rock doves are mostly confined to the north and west coasts. The double black wing bars and white rump may indicate a "pure" bred individual, although they hybridise readily with their domesticated descendants, the ubiquitous feral pigeons.

Peregrines reside in many habitats, from mountain and moorland to towering city centre buildings, but sea cliff sites are perfectly acceptable and it is always the highlight of any day to witness a flypast, either on cruise control or in plummeting attack, maybe on the aforementioned doves or pigeons.

Ravens, jackdaws and choughs may all nest if conditions are suitable in terms of site and feeding areas. So can swifts and house martins, using cliffs, crevices and caves as their ancestors did before they discovered a preference for our buildings and dwellings.

This harsh environment is suited only to the hardiest plants that cling to ledges, cracks and crevices, rooting in the thinnest scraps of soil. A firm anchor is required, however, to withstand the ceaseless winds that also threaten to dry out any vegetation, and salt laden sea spray has also to be tolerated.

Thrift is a wonderful sight around our coasts in May and June when it is in all its pink glory. The large compact cushions of its leaves provide a water proofed cover for the vulnerable soil and for its roots. It has small, narrow leaves which help to reduce water loss still further. Sea campion on the other hand has very waxy leaves that seal the water in, whilst other plants may have thick fleshy leaves that act as a reservoir of water.

Not all cliffs are stable enough to hold seabird and plant communities and the restless pounding of storm waves means that our coasts are always changing. Sometimes this happens dramatically as in the case of the Bindon landslide of 1839 in Dorset. This area, known as "The Undercliffs", is now a true wilderness area, largely untouched by man since that time and is now the best example of a naturally generated ash woodland in the UK. The dense vegetation and profusion of hart's tongue fern give it a temperate rainforest feel and it is unwise to leave the narrow path as deep holes and chasms make it dangerous to do so.

Sunlit Razorbill
Not as gregarious as puffins and guillemots   more
reticent   reserved   withdrawn   In global and UK
terms it is a fairly rare seabird   a precious gem

Balcary Heughs,
Dumfries and Galloway.
Oil

Razorbill with chick.
Balcary Heughs,
Dumfries and Galloway
Pencil

Sitting Around
A puffin topped sea stack   A glide away from ferry bound Westray   High June and sadly there was little food arriving at the burrows   Artistically there was much to savour

Puffins,
Castle O'Burrian, Westray,
Orkney.
Oil

10 SEA CLIFFS AND STACKS

Peregrine
Balcary Heughs.
Watercolour

Barafundle Bay
Immature peregrine forging a life alone   Launches full out attack on a pigeon   Plunging diving twisting   at a scarcely believable speed   Trapped together in blurring do or die mode   Locked on fast forward   Quicksilver reactions slashing acute angles into the air

   Both disappear behind a low headland only for the peregrine to emerge   empty taloned   Went briefly for a pipit in apparent frustration   before peeling away across a bruised sky to sit and rest in the upper circle of cliffs back across the bay

   I looked around the beach   No one stood open mouthed   No one applauded   There was no whooping and a hollering   There should have been whooping and a hollering   If not for the peregrine then at least for the pigeon

Peregrine, Balcary Heughs,
Dumfries and Galloway
Oil

Too Close for Comfort
The fulmar resides on the wind   Teasing lift from the waves   Hitching long distances in search of trawler discards and other surface food   Big increases in their numbers over the last century   Orkney had only one breeding pair in 1900   By the end of the century there were 90,000 pairs   Long lived birds   Up to 50 years   Loyally mating for life   Much cackling and head waving   Gape beaked threats

Fulmars, Yesnaby
Orkney.
Acrylic

Something to Shout About

Fulmar,
Balcary Heughs,
Dumfries and Galloway.
Oil

Kittiwakes
Dunbar,
East Lothian
Watercolour

14 SEA CLIFFS AND STACKS

On Eggs
There is a poignancy here   This thrift crowned sea stack should have been adorned by 30 – 40 pairs of Arctic terns incubating clutches   They had quickly abandoned any attempts to breed this year due to the lack of food in the seas around Orkney   Yet another year without any fledging terns on these islands   The oystercatchers did however look pretty in pink

Oystercatcher,
Skiba Geo, Orkney.
Acrylic

Kittiwake
Pencil

Anyone Home?

Puffin,
Castle O'Burrian,
Westray, Orkney.
Acrylic

SEA CLIFFS AND STACKS

Kittiwakes
Pencil

Wing Stretch
Smartly black and white with face painted stripes
Narrowed wings   A compromised design   More
elegant underwater than in the air

Razorbills,
Mull of Galloway,
Dumfries and Galloway.
Pastel and acrylic

The Line Up
Black guillemots are often to be found nesting in nooks and crevices towards the foot of cliffs   In certain places they nest in holes in harbour walls affording great views

Black Guillemots,
Oban Harbour,
Argyll and Bute.
Acrylic and pastel

DRAWN TO THE EDGE 21

Siblings
These three youngsters were hunkered down in the grass at the top of the cliff   Maybe just having left the large nest below   A patient wait for their parents and the next feed

Juvenile Ravens,
Meikle Ross,
Dumfries and Galloway.
Oil

Shade
A warm warm day   Much
panting and shade required
Not just me

Guillemots,
Balcary Heughs,
Dumfries and Galloway.
Oil

Guillemots,
Balcary Heughs.
Pencil

26　SEA CLIFFS AND STACKS

There is always an enjoyable sense of anticipation when you drive into the car park at Bempton Cliffs RSPB nature reserve in early summer   Spectacle guaranteed   Compellingly drawn to the cliff's edge   Want the rush of being there   Want to slow down and savour the expectancy

    Out of the visitor centre and a barn owl lands on the grass 20 feet in front of me   If I'd had any intention of rushing here was the perfect antidote   Only after I'd got over that little visual treat did other senses start to register   The guano laced air   A generally strident hubbub of noise towards the sea with discernible 'kitti-wa-a-k, kitti-wa-a-k' calls   Swirling scraps of flight form a disordered melee at the edge of the land

    Without realising it my pace quickens   I guess my pulse also   The smell intensifies   the noise reaches cacophony levels   the sea rushes to fill the expanding void   but 400 feet below   and now the whole air heaves with movement and life   the cliff face teeming with birds   What an utterly mesmerising thrilling sight

Bempton,
East Yorkshire,
Oil

Those In The Sun
Gannets
Bempton Cliffs,
East Yorkshire.
Oil

Gannets
Bempton Cliffs.
Pencil

Hanging Around

Gannet and Kittiwakes,
Bempton Cliffs, East Yorkshire.
Oil

Gannet
Bempton Cliffs,.
Pencil

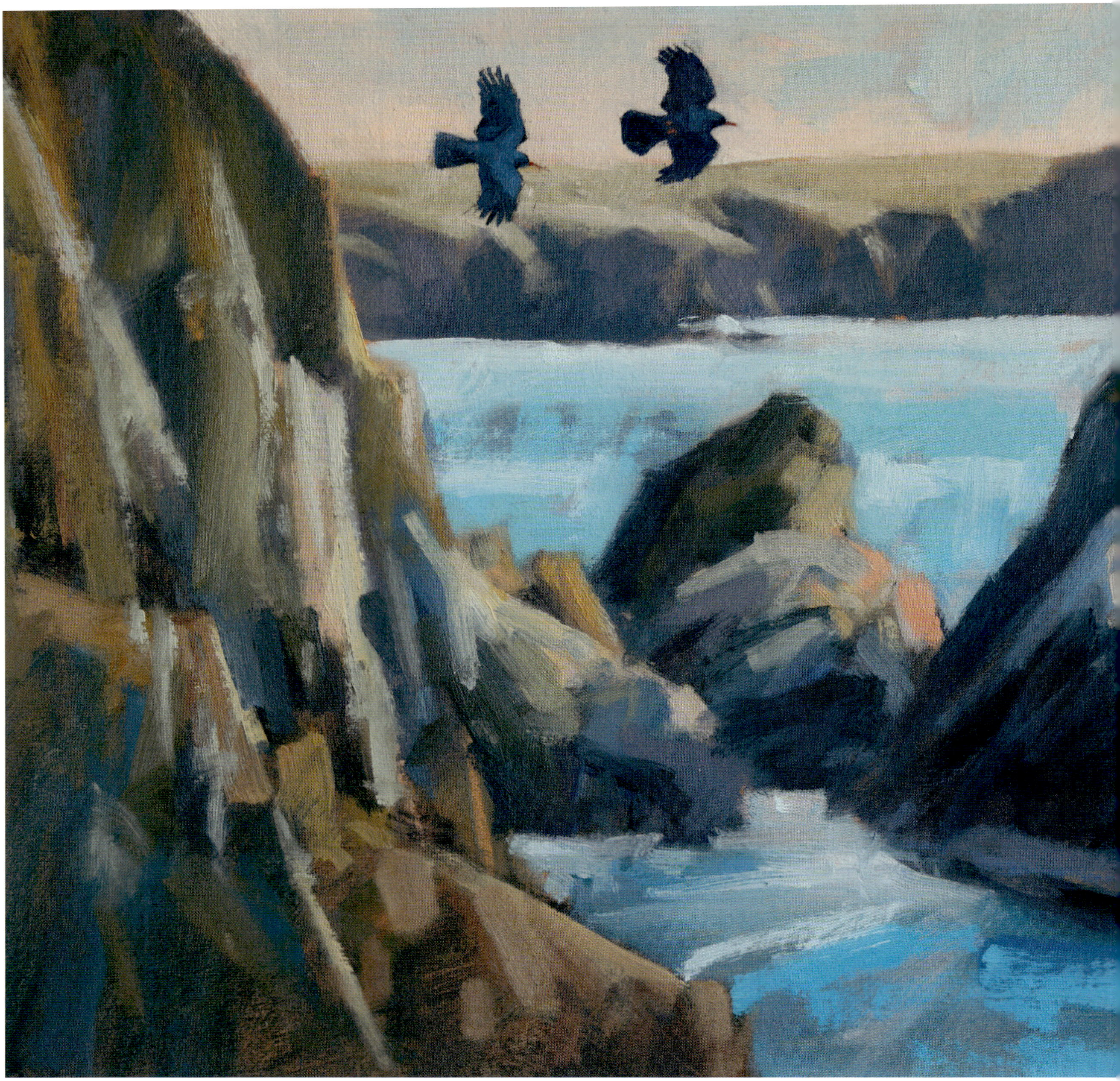

Kynance Cove

Gave the grey faced day a chance   Shuffled out along the Lizard Peninsula hoping for sunshine and choughs   The choughs have recolonized Cornwall of their own volition after a long absence   Both showed at Kynance Cove   the choughs announcing their presence with a guitar string twanging kee-ow   The sun igniting gleaming colours on the rock faces   A wind whirled vortex of gulls adorned the Lion Rock

Choughs at Kynance Cove, Cornwall.
Oil

Towards White Nothe

A raging torrent wind   roaring through gaps and gullies   Brave ragged pipits   spindrift driven   Amidst the mayhem a pair of ravens revelled   in synchronised union   Rising as weightless as wind spume   then diving gravity borne   Rolling inverted   wing tips to tail   Snapping level again with an extrovert's twist   Catching another lift before shearing away downwind with subtle wing shape shift

Ravens,
The Jurassic Coast, Dorset
Acrylic

Raven Blues
Alone on the leeward edge   a single raven   rollercoasting the cliff's wave with exhilarating ease   Discerning movements and patterns beyond our perception
Conjuring moments of grace beyond our comprehension   A supreme storm surfer   An ink blue black distillation of wind whipped air

Coul Point, Islay.
Acrylic

St. Abb's Head
Over the brow of the hill from the lighthouse car park
That small rush of fear   the involuntary snag of the breath
as the ground suddenly vanishes in front of you   The
comforting horizontals of land sea and horizon are dramatically replaced by dizzying verticals   Echoing cries
and calls corralled into this huge scooped amphitheatre
Layers of sound rushing skywards on the updraughts
falsetto kittiwakes   the throaty gargling of guillemots
Angled birds teetering on the wind

Borders
Watercolour and gouache

Deepening Shadows
Densely packed onto precariously narrow white ledges   premium rate spaces   a nebulous testy sociability
much bickering with the neighbours   noisy squabbles   vociferous multi chorused growling gargles

Guillemots
St. Abb's Head, Borders.
Acrylic

What's Going On?
There were tystie shenanigans going on below   Here in the balcony all was calm

Shag and Black Guillemot,
Brough of Birsay,
Orkney.
Oil

Paired Up

Black Guillemots,
Mull Of Galloway,
Dumfries and Galloway.
Oil

Probing Chough
A stretch of mist draped cliffs   Occasional heavy rain staining heather and wild carrot   This territory of chough pair and two eager youngsters   Frequently disturbed by walkers along the heath coast path   With time they would always return to feed again   Hunched waits beneath a dripping umbrella   Until the mist descended still further Now knee height   Retired to the car to listen to Murray – Federer in Wimbledon final   Ah well   Next time

South Stack, Anglesey.
Oil

Maritime Heath and Maritime Grassland

Choughs, South Stack, Anglesey. *Watercolour*

Maritime heaths and grasslands are found on headlands and cliff tops in western Britain, exposed to the gales and storms of the Atlantic and they form a rare habitat of international importance.

A vegetation gradient often exists away from cliff tops, as the effects of exposure to salt spray and the wind decrease. Salt tolerant plants, such as thrift and sea plantain, adorn the upper cliffs but, as conditions become less extreme back from

Sitting Pretty
Softly eidered down at the back of a grassy hollow   Tail pressed tight against the supportive rock   Camouflaged stillness her only protection   Wary eyed alertness her main defence   I sat a short distance away to draw her through the 'scope   To give her space to breathe
How long has she been sitting here?   Without food   Just courage and determination   Once her ducklings hatch she has to guide them along that precarious journey to the sea   The distance   the cliffs   aerial predators   The stark realities   The fragility

Brough of Birsay, Orkney.
Oil

the edge, herbs, sedges and grasses can grow and specialised plants such as spring squill, grass of Parnassus and, in Orkney, the Scottish primrose are all to be found. Further still from the coast, heather species begin to dominate and it is this maritime heath that provides nesting opportunities for birds such as wheatears, stonechats, linnets, skylarks, meadow pipits and twites. In the Northern Isles of Scotland this habitat is used by arctic terns and arctic skuas.

These maritime grasslands and heaths are important feeding grounds for choughs and here some grazing can be crucial. On Old Lizard Head in Cornwall, where choughs have recolonised of their own volition, an area of grassland is grazed by sure footed Shetland ponies. The cropped grass and pony dung provide ideal feeding conditions for these charismatic corvids.

Preening Chough

South Stack, Anglesey.
Oil

Twites
Breeding on coastal heaths   as well as upland
moors and mountains   Feeding on saltmarsh and
strandlines to get through the winter

Hobbister,
Orkney.
Oil

Chough,
South Stack,
Anglesey.
Pencil

MARITIME HEATH AND MARITIME GRASSLAND

Arctic Skua
Yesnaby,
Orkney.
Watercolour

Arctic Skuas
I was looking forward to being assaulted by skuas   never having undergone the experience   Despite the birds being paired up on territory   and dark phase birds will pair with light phase birds   they had nothing to defend   no nest or eggs   Arctic skuas are piratical   stealing fish from terns kittiwakes and auks   These groups of birds are faring poorly on Orkney   no fish to steal   no point in even attempting to lay any eggs   The arctic skua may be gone as a breeding bird in Britain within just a few years

Yesnaby,
Orkney.
Oil

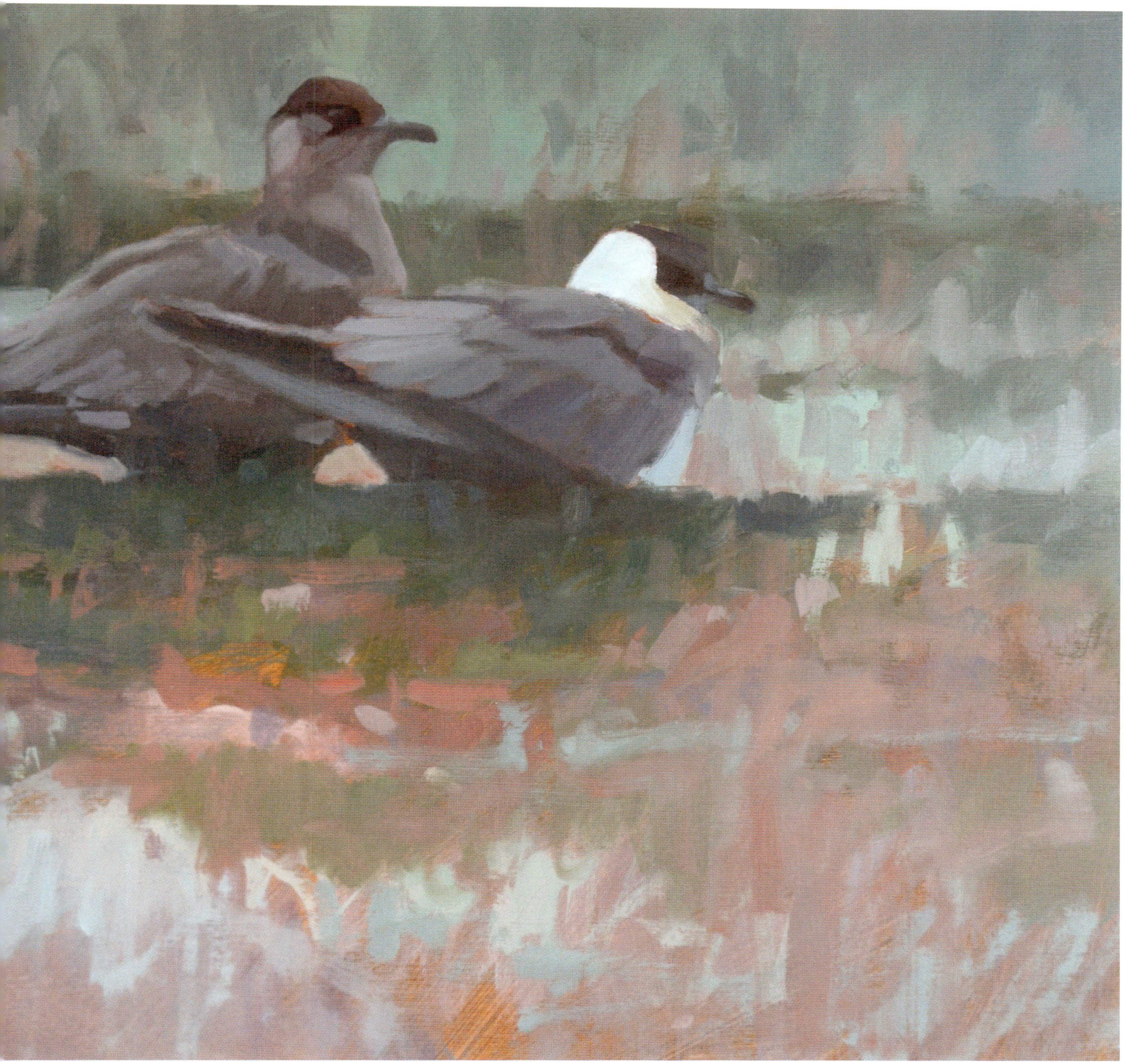

Solway Shore,
Southerness, Dumfries and Galloway.
Watercolour

Rocky Shores

Rocky shores make up the most common coastal habitat in Britain, yet the sea scoured nature of these hard edges appears to yield few dependable sites for wildlife to cling to. However, the protection afforded by crevices and gulleys and by foreshore pools and boulders gives specialist fauna and flora the chance to grow and breed.

On Alert

Head Down   Drawing roosting waders through the
'scope   Later   looking around to see what I might
be missing   This eye-leveled peregrine   Not even
30 metres distant   How long have you been there?
Uncompromisingly indifferent to my presence
More important matters to hand
After quite some time of total concentration on both
our parts it was away   Determinedly fast and low
Slicing apart the morning

Peregrine, Southerness, Dumfries and Galloway.
Pastel

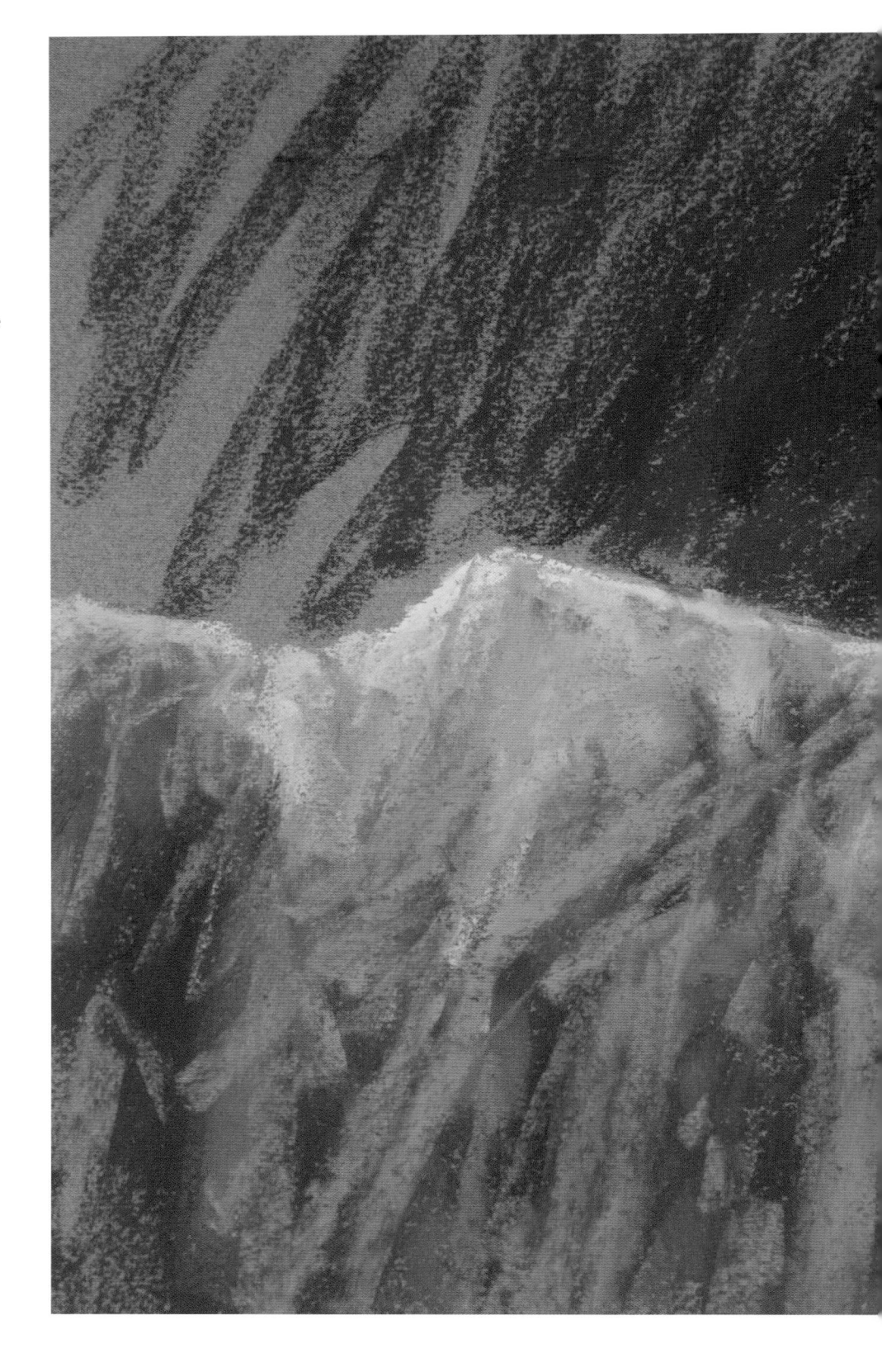

DRAWN TO THE EDGE   51

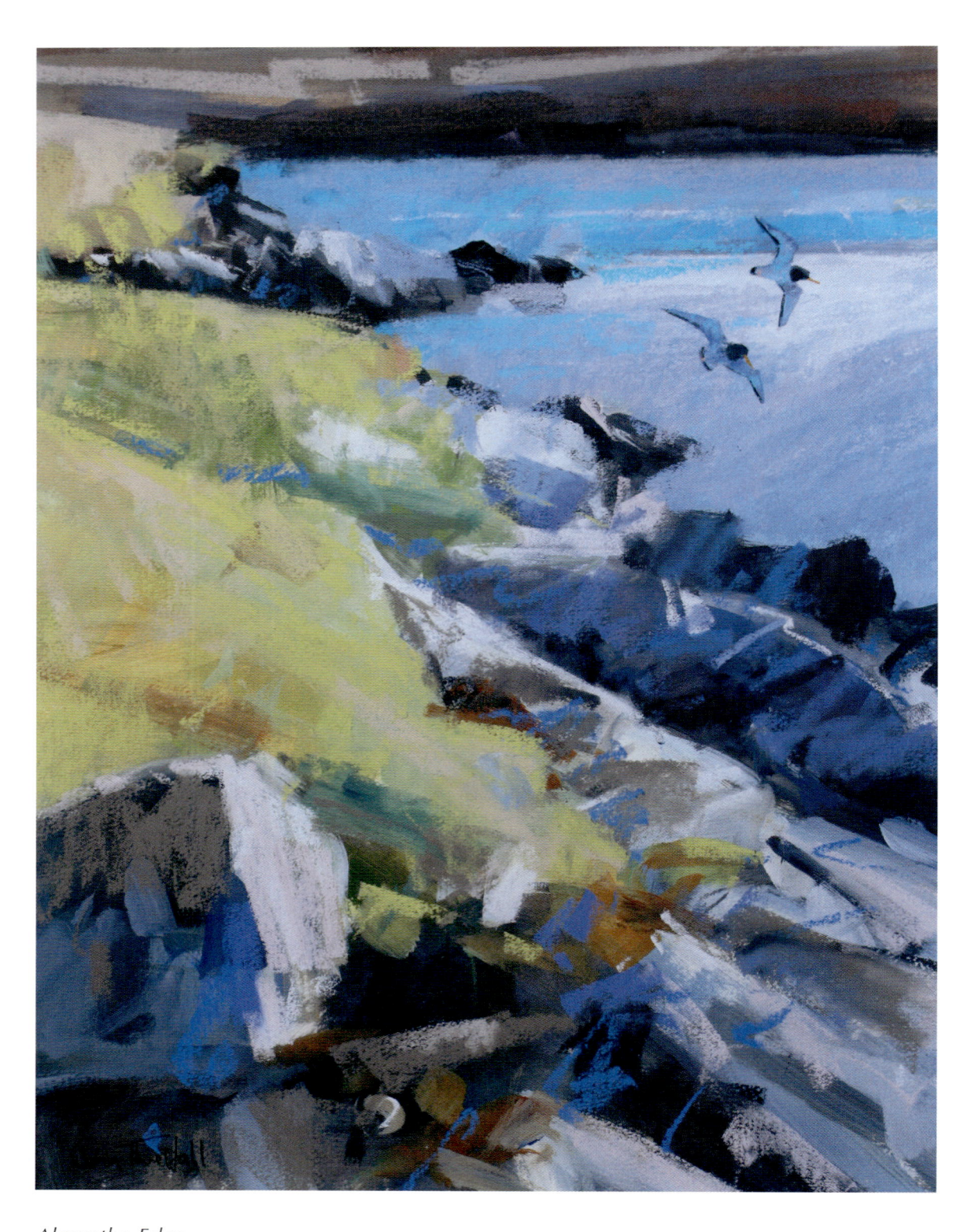

Along the Edge
I'd just fallen into a river attempting to escort our elderly dog across some haphazard stepping stones   As the sun made a welcome appearance I was keen to stop and sort myself out   Immune to my discomfort two oystercatchers chased along the edge of this inlet   As noisy as ever   Fragments of sea urchin shell on the lochside rocks   Otters must be around here somewhere   Probably watching me wring out my socks

Loch Euphort, North Uist, Outer Hebrides.
Acrylic and Pastel

Kingfisher, Rockliffe.
Pencil

Sandwich Tern,
Southerness.
Watercolour

DRAWN TO THE EDGE 53

Common Seals

All would be tranquil and siesta like for long snoozing stretched out minutes   Suddenly on some unspecified trigger or impulse   they all crash into the water   a loud wake of sound arriving after the event   followed by much seal play and messing about   then it was time to haul out again   Much settling   stretching and scratching

Kildonan,
Isle of Arran.
Oil

Seaweeds are the most familiar plants on rocky shores. These algae have to withstand dramatic extremes of environmental conditions; twice daily immersion in salt water and subsequent exposure to dessicating winds or drenching rains or freezing temperatures or high heat and humidity. The less resilient species are found lower down the shore, where they are exposed to the air for less periods of time. The tougher species are able to withstand conditions higher up the shore, where, not only are they exposed for longer, but they face wave action that can often be intense.

This zonation in general is in fact a characteristic of rocky shores and is particularly evident at low tide. The highest zone, or splash zone, is dominated by lichens, often a stripe of orange lichen above a deep band of black.

Purple Sandpiper

I know the purple sandpipers are there   I just cannot find them until the rising tide nudges them out of the rocks eases them into view   for which I am grateful

With Turnstones, Southerness,
Dumfries and Galloway.
Oil

Purple Sandpipers

Southerness,
Dumfries and Galloway.
Oil

The upper shore can take a wave battering at high tide but there will also be times in the tidal cycle when this zone is not covered at all. Animal species here, such as limpets and barnacles, tend to have hard shells for protection.

The rocks of the middle zone will be covered by each high tide but with the constant ebb and flow of the water will suffer from much abrasion. Animals here have to be hard shelled but must also be able to anchor themselves firmly to the rocks, as do mussels for example, or hard shelled and mobile, able to seek refuge under the seaweed or in crevices, as are winkles and topshells. Some soft bodied creatures, such as anemones, may be found in this zone, but require the extra protection afforded by rock pools that do not dry out.

In the lowest zone, species are exposed for the least amount of time and here the diversity is greater. The rock pools are larger and deeper, harbouring prawns and shrimps, shannies and gobies, sea slugs and squirts, cowries and crabs.

Of the bird species, the rock pipit is the most adapted, nesting in crevices above the high tide line and feeding on insects and sandhoppers. During the winter months, turnstones and purple sandpipers hunt for small crustaceans and molluscs among the rocks and seaweeds.

Both species of seal frequent these rocky shores, hauling out for seal siestas or, in June for the common or harbour seal and in November for the grey seal, using undisturbed shores and coves to give birth to their pups.

Particularly in the north and west, otters can be found hunting for fish and larger crustaceans.

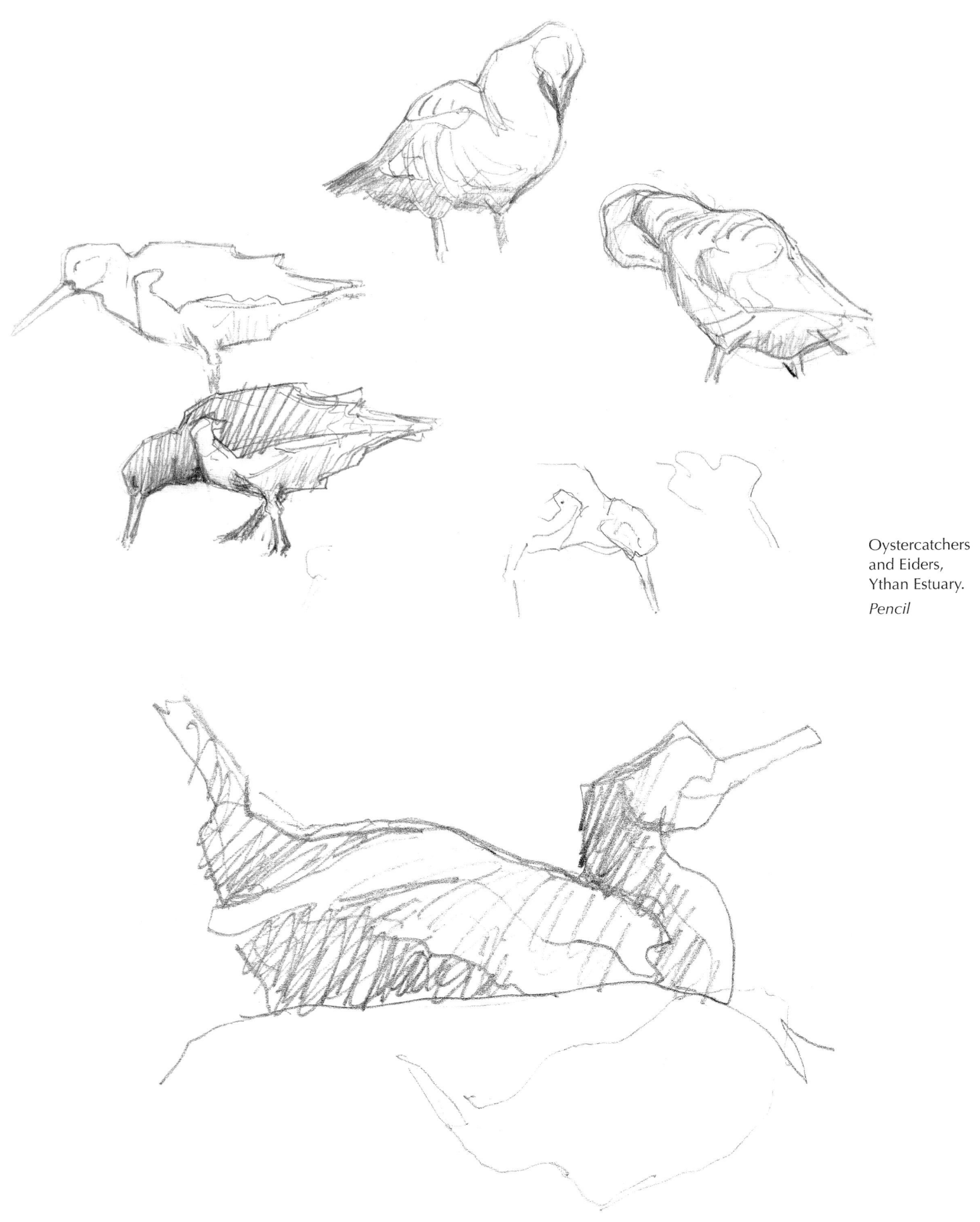

Oystercatchers and Eiders, Ythan Estuary.
Pencil

Flitting Wheatear
Autumn prone wheatears everywhere   Trending south
Each and every one of them a delight to the eye

Lagan Arnal, North Uist
Outer Hebrides.
Oil (detail)

Mull Goat

The Carsaig coastline   Squeezed between the hard edged sea and the high crafted cliffs   Free range goats forage   Smell them before seeing them

Carsaig,
Isle of Mull.
Oil

Coastal Goats

Carsaig,
Isle of Mull.
Oil

Turnstone

A turnstone's winter transformation   From head down low profile subtleties   to the males white headed and masked   chestnut and black backed bravado of spring leaving our shores in peak condition for the rituals of northern latitudes

Southerness,
Dumfries and Galloway.
Oil

Rock Pipit
Just sat there   Relishing the final warmth of the day

Yesnaby, Orkney.
Oil

62   ROCKY SHORES

Turnstones,
Southerness.
Pencil

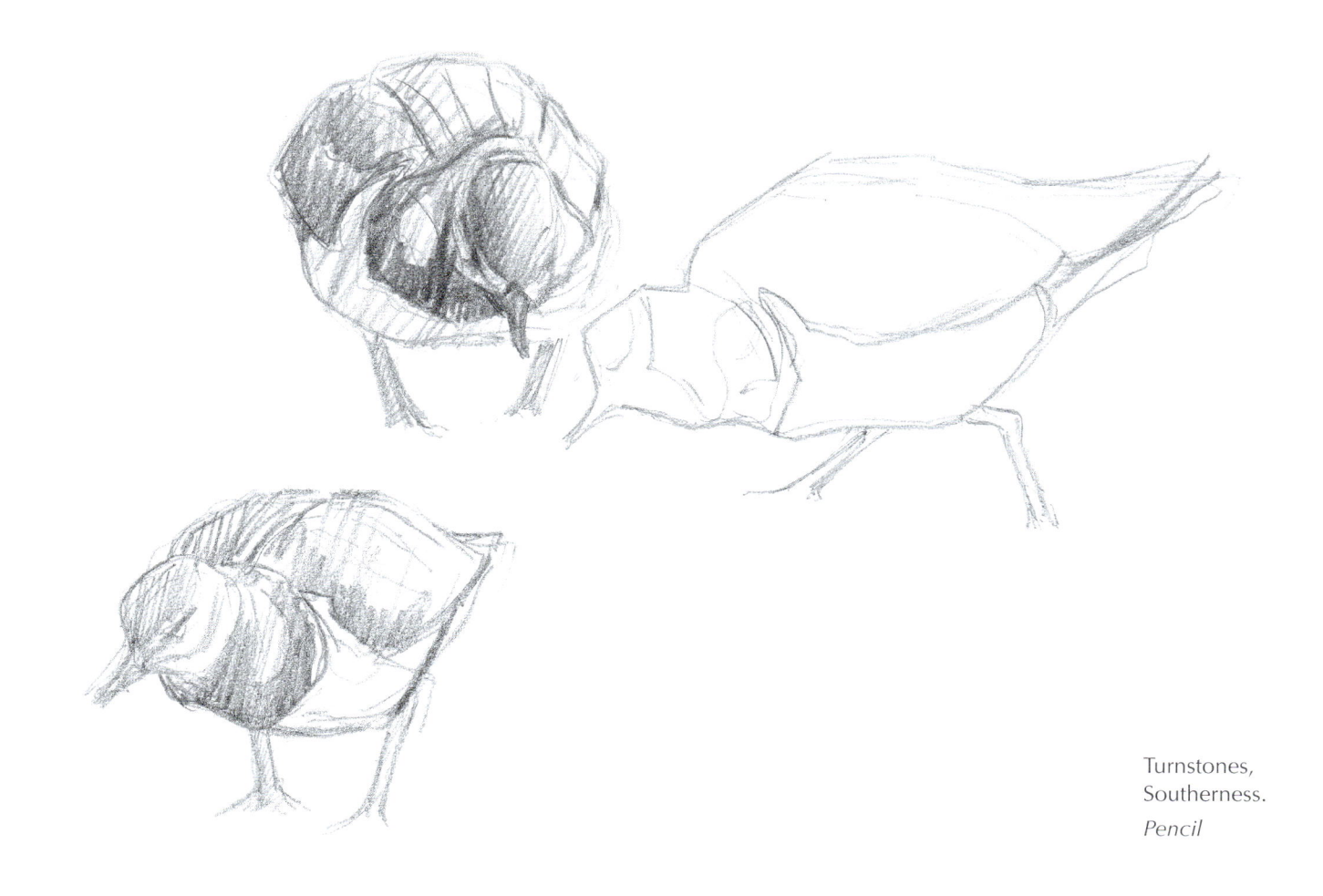

Turnstones

Wigg Bay, Loch Ryan,
Dumfries and Galloway.
Oil

Dunlin with Turnstones

Wigg Bay, Loch Ryan,
Dumfries and Galloway.
Oil

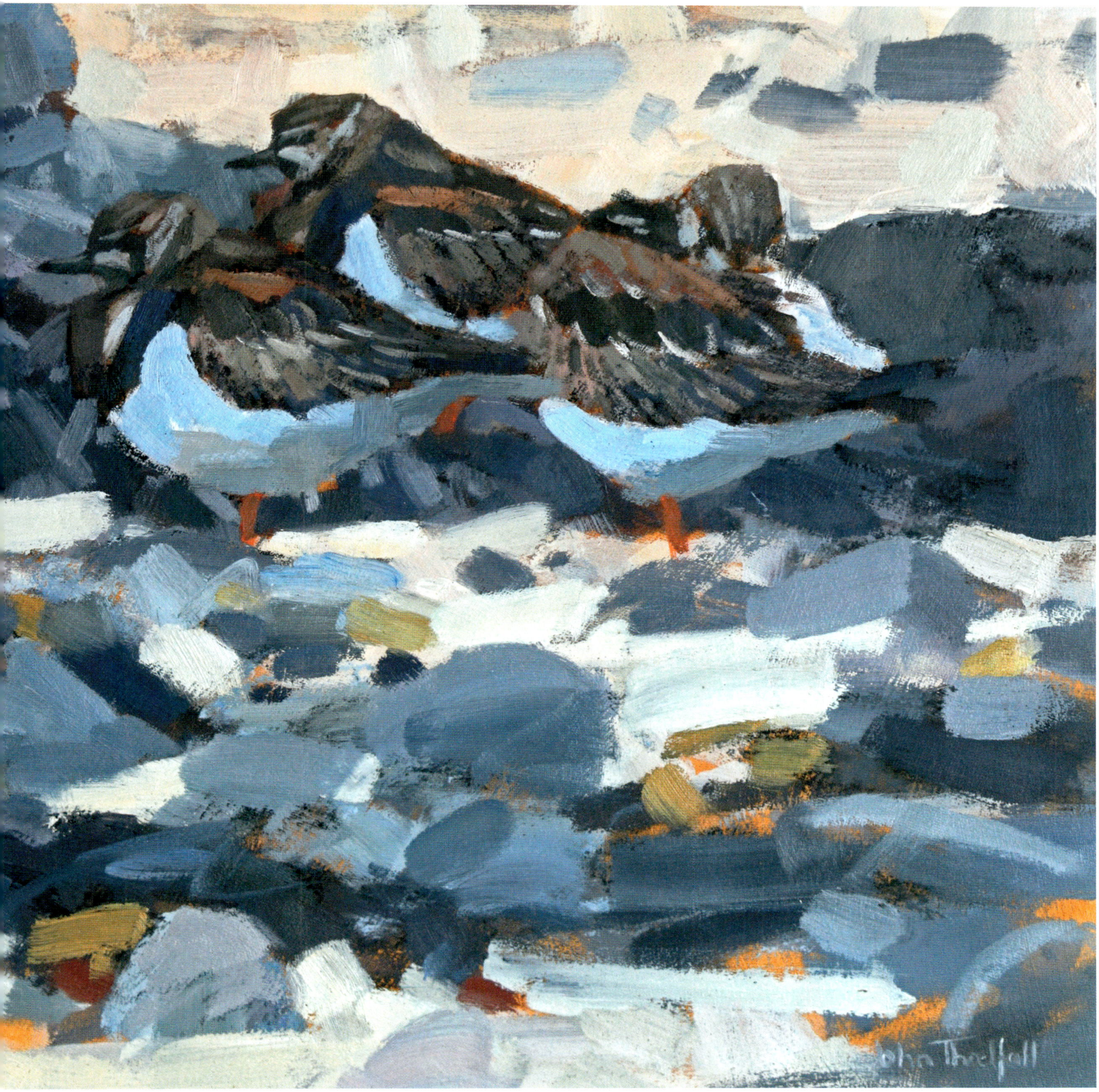
ohn Threlfall

Arran Otter
A windless horizonless calm   shimmeringly warm whelmingly bright   A becalmed otter on this skyless morning   An occasional sniff   stretch   and scratch

Kildonan, Isle of Arran.
Oil

DRAWN TO THE EDGE 67

Bouldery Beach
This wave and weather pummelled headland shattered bedrock contrasting with smooth rolled boulders

Rubha Sgeir nan Sgarbh,
Isle of Harris.
Acrylic

Over Southerness
The ramrod straight flight of the cormorant
The daily commute

Cormorants, Southerness,
Dumfries and Galloway.
Oil

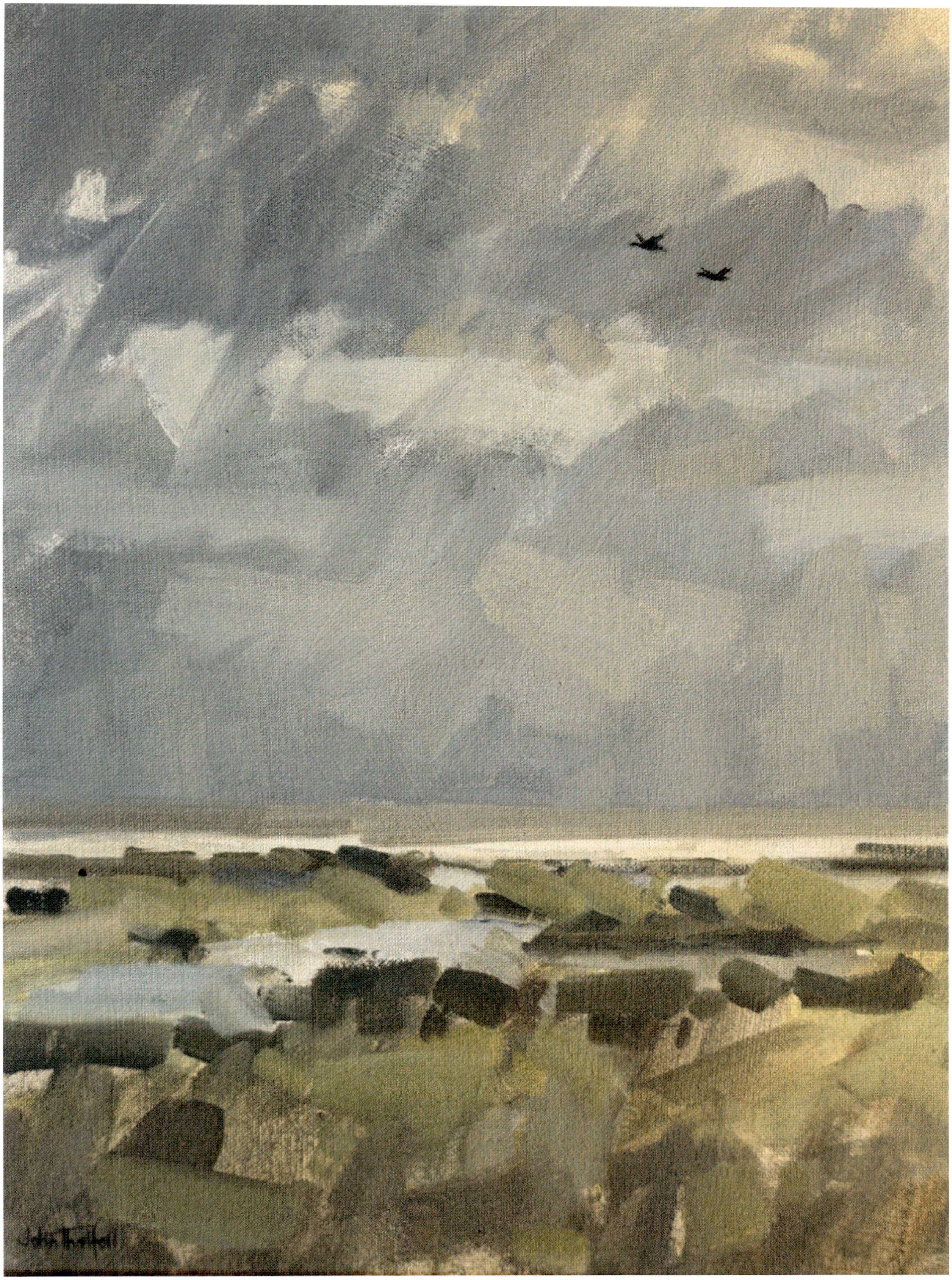
John Threlfall

Male Eoder
Ythan,
Watercolour

70   ROCKY SHORES

DRAWN TO THE EDGE   71

Rocky Cove
Any calls from the seals drowned out by the wave crashing echoing cove

Grey Seals,
Marloes, Pembrokeshire.
Oil

My Pool
'It's back' I impulsively shout out   and then realise there is no one within ear shot   Only during a prolonged spell of very cold weather do we seem to get kingfishers on our stretch of coast   As soon as it warms slightly again they are away   Would love to know where   Frequently it is just a male bird and he has his favourite perch above his favourite rock pool   Knowing where to look means I can monitor his presence even from the road   If the temperatures plummet once more I know he will be back

Kingfisher,
Rockcliffe, Dumfries and Galloway.
Oil

Common Seals,
Kildonan, Arran.
Watercolour

Displaying Mergansers

Red-breasted Mergansers,
Lamlash, Isle of Arran.
Oil

Juvenile Shag,
Isle of Arran
Pencil

Juvenile Shag,
Isle of Arran
Watercolour

Juvenile Shag

Clauchlands Point,
Isle of Arran.
Oil

Schrodinger's Seal

The battle scarred headland of the Waternish peninsula ends in consternation   wary and distrusting of that heavy leaden sea   A flotilla of fire forged skerries are aligned offshore   like basaltic tug boats   Unconcerned grey seals bobbing   bottle nosed   somnolent   Except one that is buoyantly curious   Gifts me a Schrodinger of a dilemma

I have to leave   It's getting late   Many moorland miles home to be crossed   I have to stay   Caught by that softly dark compelling gaze at this our species interface   Stretching arcs of awareness to span a few yards of taut salty space   Dripping whiskers the only mark of time

I made my choice and the world split   I left and remain undeniably indifferent   I stayed and remain undeniably changed

Grey Seal
Waternish, Isle of Skye.
Oil

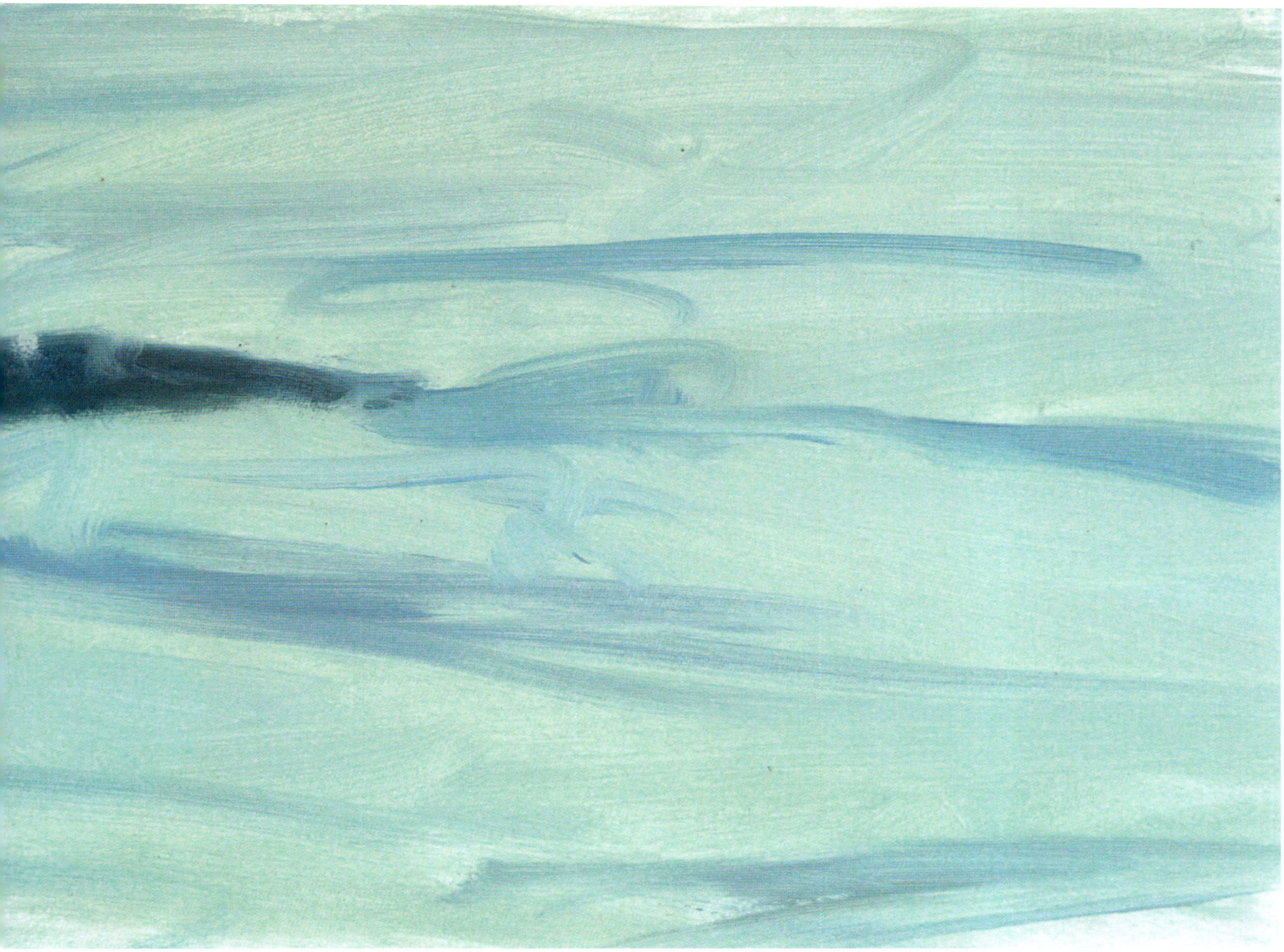

Little Terns
Foulney Island, Cumbria.
Watercolour

Shingle

Little Terns
Foulney Island, Cumbria.
Watercolour

Looking at an Ordnance Survey map of the Dorset coast, one feature stands out above all others, the apparently ruler straight line of Chesil Beach and, sheltering behind it for more than half its length, the Fleet Lagoon.

On the ground, Chesil Beach is even more remarkable, a huge barrier bank of pebbles 18 miles long, up to 200 metres wide and 13 metres in height, making it the most extensive accumulation of shingle in the world.

Ringed Plover
The early summer weather of 2012 on the Farne Islands was torrentially bad. Many many pufflings were drowned in their burrows as they succumbed to flooding

Cemlyn Bay,
Anglesey.
Acrylic and Oil

Furthermore, those pebbles are graded, from pea sized in the west, beneath the sand warm corrugated cliffs of West Bay, to baked potato sized in the east as the bank aborts against the immovable object that is the Isle of Portland. The incessant pounding of the waves has rounded the rock fragments and even the largest pebbles move in stormy seas, in the process of movement and sorting along the coast. This "longshore drift" has created other notable shingle spits and bars such as Orford Ness in Suffolk and Foulness Point in Essex.

This unstable and seemingly barren habitat would appear to be inhospitable to any form of wildlife. The seaward side would indeed tend to be devoid of vegetation but the landward side of a shingle bank, or areas above the high tide zone, may acquire enough stability to allow some specialist plants to colonise. Sea kale, sea pea, sea campion, curled dock, viper's bugloss and yellow horned poppy are just some of the plants that can thrive in such arid, salt laden, nutrient poor conditions. These colonised areas in turn provide feeding opportunities for birds.

SHINGLE

Can't See Me
Raised shell beach   I'm hoping that there aren't going to be any unexpectedly high tides in the next wee while   or crows or gulls   or stoats   or rats   or dogs   or

Mersehead,
Dumfries and Galloway.
Acrylic

Little Tern
Foulney Island, Cumbria.
Watercolour

There are few birds that choose to nest on shingle. Ringed plovers and oystercatchers are exceptions, as are a number of tern species. Shingle is in fact the most important nesting habitat for little terns in the UK. Arctic, common and Sandwich terns will all use shingle to raise their young.

Disturbance and predation are big problems for such ground nesting birds. With fewer than 2,000 pairs this is of particular conservation concern for the little tern. Fencing may keep out mammalian predators such as fox, hedgehog and stoat, as well as alerting walkers, with or without dogs, to the sensitivity of the site, but aerial predation by large gulls, crows and kestrels is more difficult to deal with.

Shingle and gravel extraction is a significant threat to this unique habitat.

Little Tern
Foulney Island, Cumbria.
Watercolour

86 SHINGLE

Little Terns

Foulney Island is only an island at high tide so the nesting area of the terns on the exposed shingle   is fenced off to deter ground predators   This does not discourage aerial predators however and a number of the nests had already lost their clutch of eggs   I was reassured that the terns would lay again

With Ringed Plover,
Foulney Island,
Cumbria.
Oil

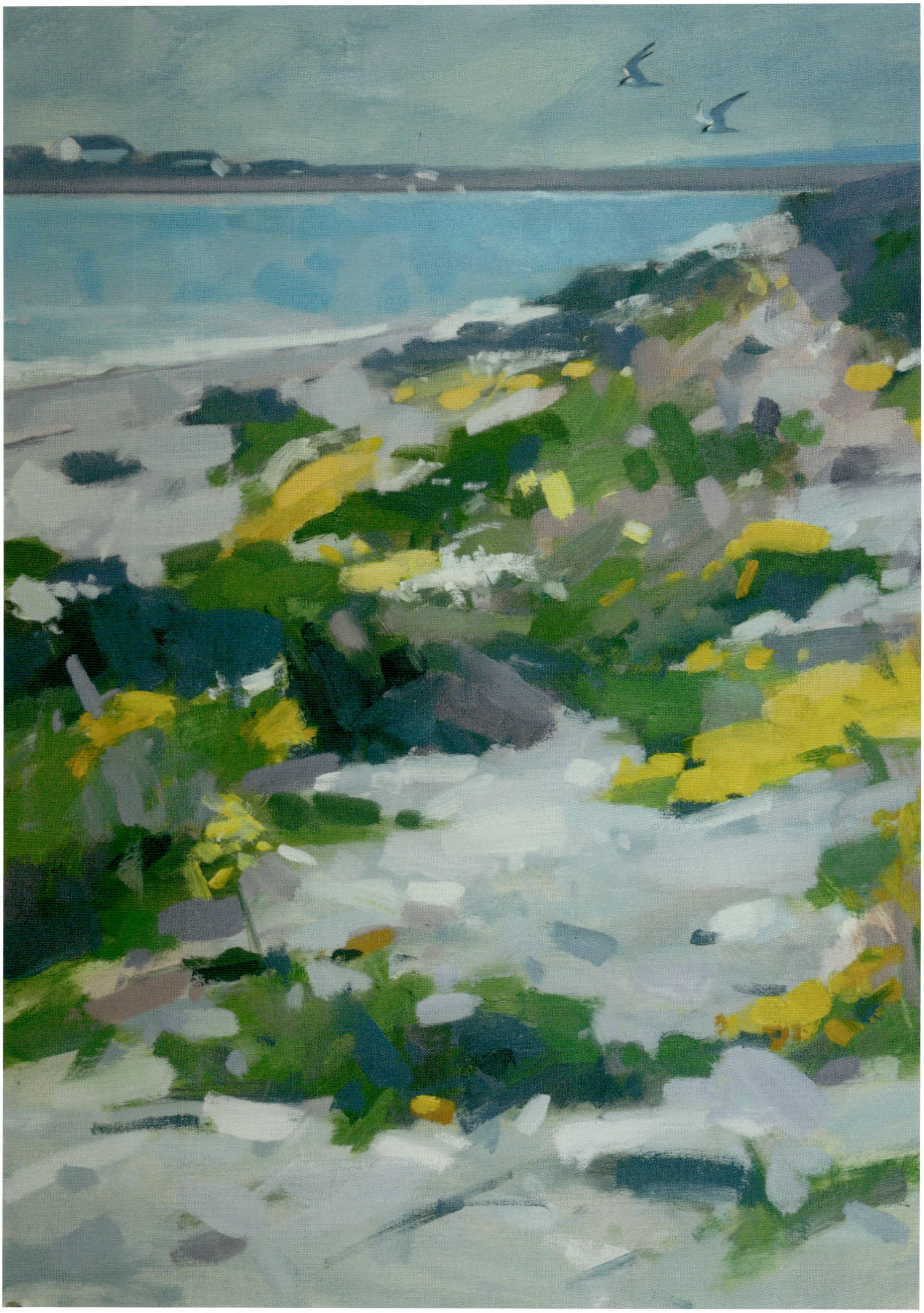

Shingle Flora
A surprisingly colourful mix of plants on this unstable
base   Little terns constantly busy   back and forth

Little Terns,
Foulney Island,
Cumbria
Oil

Sandwich Terns,
Cemlyn Bay.
Pencil

90 SALINE LAGOONS

Saline Lagoons

So Demanding
You try your best to ignore them   and they just won't let you

Sandwich Terns,
Cemlyn Bay, Anglesey.
Oil

The Fleet in Dorset is the largest tidal lagoon in Britain, but so sheltered is it by the enormity of Chesil Beach that this elongated stretch of water varies considerably along its length. It is indeed saline towards its eastern end where it connects to the sea, via a narrow channel, into Portland

Posturing Terns

Sandwich Terns,
Cemlyn Bay, Anglesey.
Acrylic on paper

DRAWN TO THE EDGE   93

Harbour. Here the tidal currents are strong but this influence diminishes on moving west, as does the salinity, until at the other extreme it is almost fresh water with no tidal influence. The diversity of life that this contrasting habitat can support is far ranging, both below and above water level.

The saline lagoon at Cemlyn Bay on Anglesey is on a much smaller scale. It was partially formed

Family Commotion

Common Terns,
Cemlyn Bay, Anglesey
Oil

by a huge storm in the 19th century that "threw" a shingle barrier across the bay. Construction of a weir in the 1930s completed the job and allowed water levels to be controlled. The islands in the lagoon now support a large breeding colony of terns of national importance.

Sandwich Tern
Cemlyn Bay, Anglesey.
Watercolour

DRAWN TO THE EDGE   97

The Fleet
A miniature inland sea   fresh water at its western end
estuarine at its eastern end   A haven for a wide diversity
of wildlife

Dorset.
Oil

Sandwich Tern
Cemlyn Bay, Anglesey.
Pencil

Sandwich Tern
Cemlyn Bay, Anglesey
Watercolour

DRAWN TO THE EDGE

Dune

Mersehead,
Dumfries and Galloway.
Pastel

Sandy Beaches and Dunes

Gull Wave

Bamburgh, Northumberland.
Acrylic

Unevenly stitched around the entire UK coast are treasured beaches that lure people back time and again. There are small, enclosed gems such as Barafundle Bay in Pembrokeshire, and glistening white stretches of Hebridean coast curving into the fading distance, with no one else in sight.

Beyond the Breakers

Acrylic

Gannet Waves

The Outer Hebrides are justly famed for their white sandy beaches   Reaching into the sea   The sharp cold clear water turned a tropical turquoise   A lone gannet arcing transects beyond the foaming breakers

Traigh Iar, Isle of Harris
Outer Hebrides.
Acrylic

Gannet Waves   Traigh Iar, Isle of Harris, Outer Hebrides. *Acrylic*

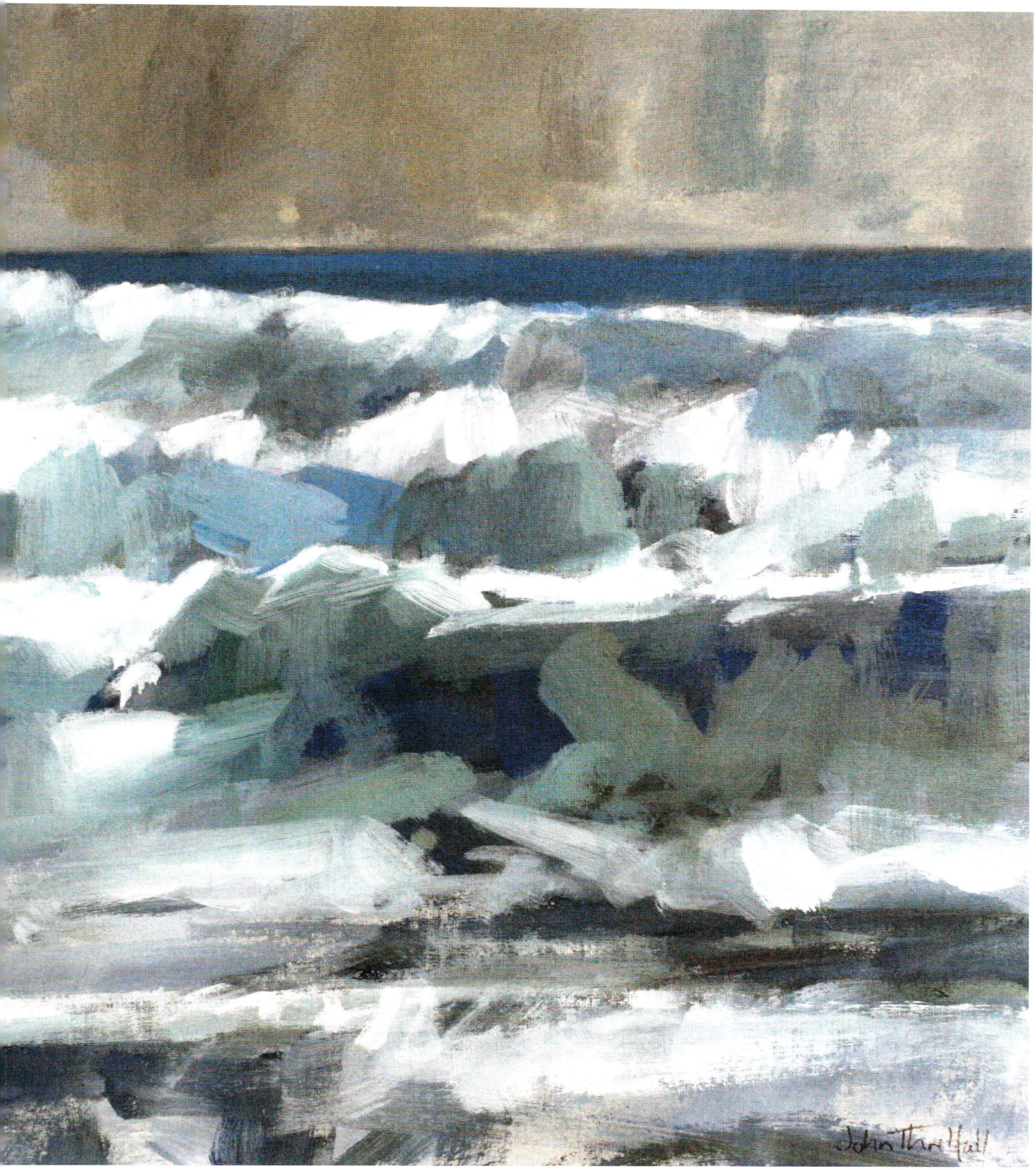
John Threlfall

Dune Backed Beach

Traigh Iar, North Uist
Outer Hebrides.
Oil

106 SANDY BEACHES AND DUNES

Cliffs, rocks, shingle and shells are gradually worn into finer and finer fragments by the power of the waves, forming sandy beaches and bays. The sea and surging tides bring in abundant food for marine invertebrates that protect themselves by burrowing into the sand at low tide. These in turn provide food for the marauding masked crab or for probing waders such as fleet footed sanderlings.

Each high tide produces a strandline of organic material, very commonly seaweeds, which slowly decays, serving as protection and food for small crustaceans such as sandhoppers. Turnstones can be seen vigorously tossing aside this debris to feed on the larder. Starlings, pied wagtails and any number of other species of bird may also be present.

Only the shortest breath of a breeze is necessary to move the finer sand particles on the beach and stronger winds prompt the whole top surface to weave downwind like smoking, whispering tendrils, scouring exposed objects and random features of flotsam and jetsam, leaving a comet's tail of sand on the leeward side. Embryonic dunes begin to develop in this way along the strandline vegetation giving an opportunity for perennial dune forming grasses, such as lyme grass, sand couch and marram, to root. These grasses have long rhizomes that help to bind and stabilise the sand allowing the dunes to grow further. The seeds of these grasses sustain snow buntings, shore larks and various finches throughout the winter.

Successive ridges of dunes may develop over time and the sheltered hollows in between, or dune slacks, have a micro climate and vegetation of their own, supporting a wide range of rare plants, invertebrates, reptiles and amphibians. The rare and protected natterjack toad is to be found here. Eiders, shelduck, terns and gulls may all nest in this dune habitat.

Farther inland, the influence of the sea diminishes, the organic content of the sand increases and dune grasslands may dominate. Plants such as bird's foot trefoil, common vetch and meadow saxifrage flourish, attracting butterflies and day flying moths.

Continuing the progression, areas of scrub take root, with sea buckthorn prominent. These bushes and small trees produce nutritious berries in the autumn and nest sites for small birds in the spring.

Passing Mergansers
 I am just imagining the mergansers' view   It was as if they had gone over for a closer look   Would love to see grey seals that close   from below whiskered levels

Sands of Forvie,
North East Scotland.
Oil

DRAWN TO THE EDGE 109

Iceland Gull
Had travelled to Fraserburgh on the strength of its reputation as a hotspot for wintering white-winged gulls   Fish factories and sewage outfall   that sort of thing   Weather wet and windy   Head for a seafront car park   30 metres from the promenade railings   A gathering of gulls on the beach   Yep   2 Iceland gulls and a glaucous gull   Large promenade shelter gives great protection from the elements for drawing and painting   Good café less than 50 metres away provides all other essentials   Wouldn't want it as simple as this all the time   I think

Third winter Iceland Gull,
Fraserburgh, North East Scotland
Watercolour

Iceland Gull study 2
See 34 (page 107)

Fraserburgh,
North East Scotland
Watercolour and Pencil

Foraging Sanderling

Ythan Estuary,
North East Scotland.
Mixed Media

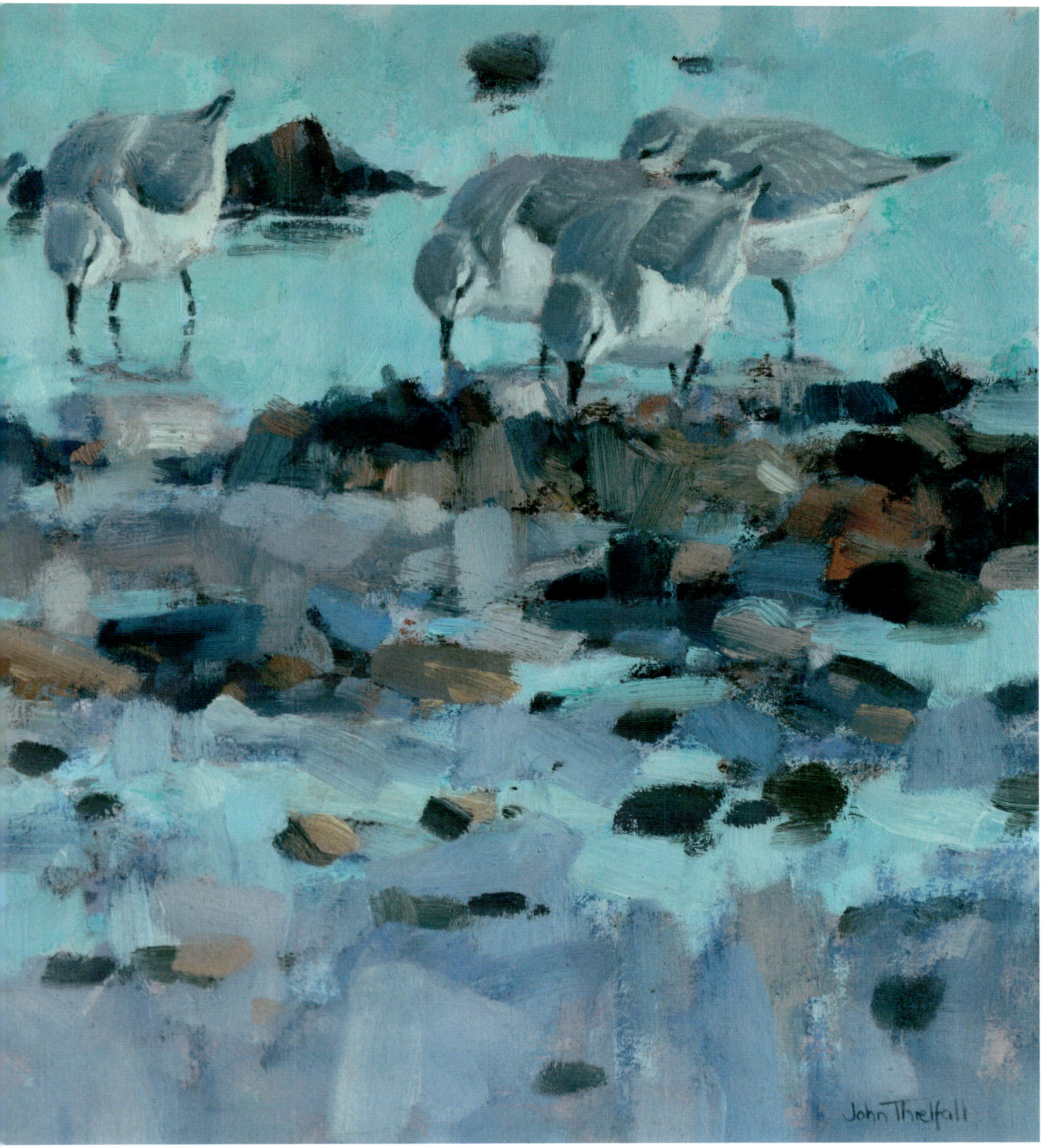
John Threlfall

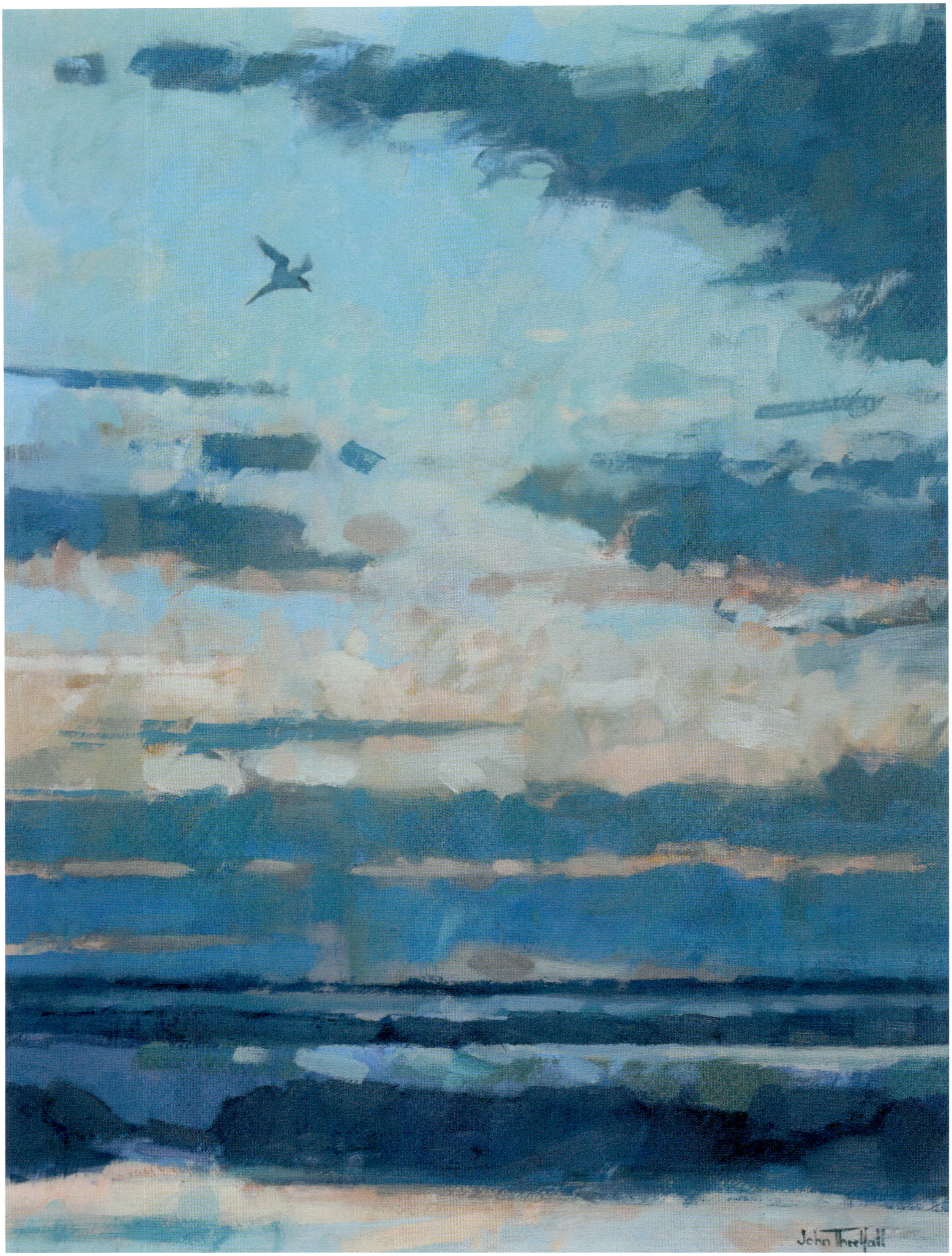
John Threlfall

Braunton Sands

To reach this beach entails a switchback walk through the wide dune system of Braunton Burrows National Nature Reserve   A mix and mosaic of micro habitats that demands exploration

Braunton,
Devon.
Pastel sketch

The Late Shift (p76)

The shallowing sea emptying into beached pools   Hovering still on the day's edge of twilight   Hungry mouths to feed

Arctic Tern, Bamburgh
Northumberland.
Mixed Media

Standing Proud
A dune colony of breeding gulls   harsh strident raucous
calls   mass ranked   intimidating

Lesser Black-backed Gulls,
Walney Island,
Cumbria.
Oil

Beach Walk

Newgale Beach,
Pembrokeshire.
Oil

Winter Light – Common Gull
Light   and water   and bird   The alchemy   The magic

Rockcliffe,
Dumfries and Galloway.
Oil

Nesting Tern

Little Tern,
Barrier Beach,
South Ronaldsay.

Watercolour and Pencil

Taking Flight
Against the backdrop of Holkham's dark pines a flurry of back lit snow buntings   Their bouncing undulating flowing flight enriches any winters day along the coast

Snow Buntings,
Holkham, Norfolk.
Oil

Snow Buntings

This confiding pair tolerated my close and prolonged proximity   hopping in and out of the marram grass at the top of the dunes to feed   They breed further into the Arctic than any other bird of comparable size   So small within the vast scheme of things   so crucial to the whole fabric of existence

Snow Buntings,
Holkham Dunes, Norfolk.
Oil

Shore Larks
On a fine winter's day there are just too many people and dogs around   the birds constantly having to move off   Best to go when it's dull and wet and sit there in the rain trying to sketch on sodden paper because I'd forgotten to take an umbrella   At least the birds didn't seem to mind   foraging for seeds   Mind you these are stunning autumn and winter visitors that you would happily sit in the rain to watch

Holkham,
Norfolk,
Oil

DRAWN TO THE EDGE 123

It's Off To Work We Go
A scurrying troupe of sanderlings   sprinting down to the water's edge   hoping to snatch a washed in morsel   rushing back up the beach before the next wave   Reluctant to get their feet wet   A bit like myself although a lot quicker

Sanderlings
Culla, Benbecula,
Outer Hebrides.
Oil

DRAWN TO THE EDGE 125

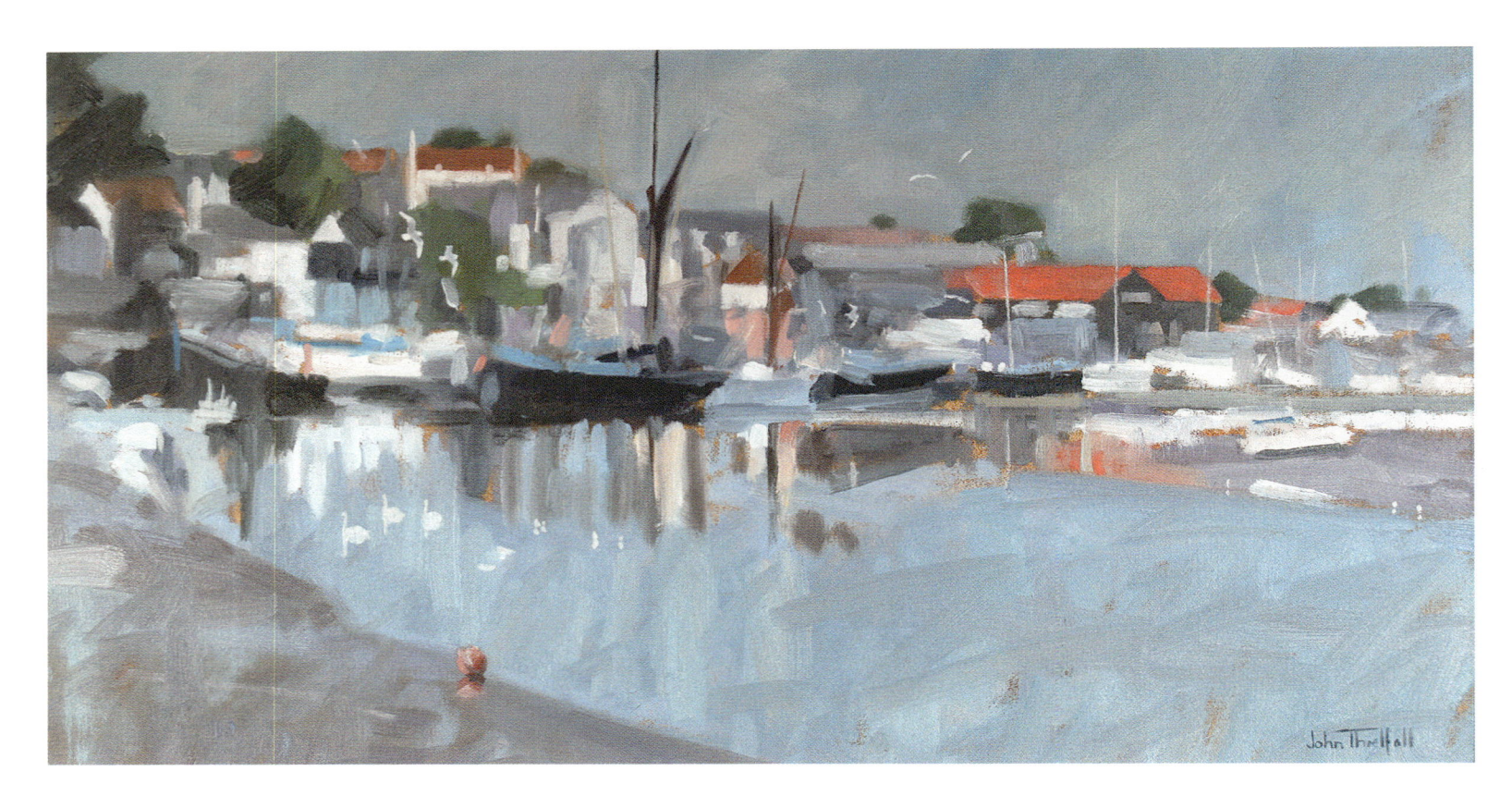

Mediterranean Gulls
A couple of Mediterranean gulls charm a light bright coloured day   Roof tops and barge sail reds   Trim and tarpaulin blues   Yacht and swan whites   Boats birds and buildings in picture harmony

Maldon, Essex.
Oil

Estuaries and Saltmarsh

Feeding Brents
OK so I've exaggerated the saltmarsh colours a bit here and abstracted the vegetation there   but

Morston, North Norfolk.
Acrylic

In terms of biomass, estuary mud is one of the most productive habitats on the planet. This is a harsh environment, however, chemically and physically, and the number of species is low, but the organic and mineral nutrient content of the mud, brought in by the tides and rivers, is extraor-

Aberlady Bay

Passing Osprey,
Aberlady Bay, East Lothian.
Oil

dinarily high, so that species that have adapted to live here occur in vast numbers.

The base of the food chain consists of surface layer algae and bacteria and the zooplankton which washes in on each tide. These in turn provide food for the creatures that live in the mud, burrowing down into the oozing softness to give themselves some defence and protection. Top layer species need to be hard shelled and these range from tiny hydrobia snails to siphon feeders such as cockles and Baltic tellins. The mud surface will be peppered with casts that betray the presence of lugworms living deep below in U-shaped burrows. Eel grass species find a sufficiently secure anchor in the mud to flourish and the bright green algae, *Enteromorpha*, is common.

Despite this huge larder, our estuaries may seem surprisingly quiet during the summer months. A lack of nest sites, and the twice daily inundation of the tides, ensure that breeding possibilities are low. Even on the bordering saltmarsh the threat of flooding is always present. The redshank may be the only bird on the lower marsh, since its chicks are able to float, while skylark, meadow pipit and linnet chance their luck on the upper reaches of the marsh. Grey herons and shelducks may feed in the creeks and swallows and martins skim the low vegetation for insects.

The saltmarsh, or merse in Scotland, however, is a wonderful sight in summer when the sea lavender blooms and the daisy like sea aster shows, and all seems peaceful and serene.

The atmosphere changes completely come the late summer and autumn, as millions of waders and wildfowl descend upon Britain's estuaries to feed, rest and moult. Many of them will move on south but many will stay on around our shores until the spring, taking advantage of the abundant

Pacing Gull

Common Gull,
Rockcliffe, Dumfries and Galloway
Oil

food supply. There is no finer sight than a low sun on gleaming mud beneath a glowering winter sky as a fitting stage for the instinctively choreographed shoals of knots and dunlins, flashing light and dark as they twistingly morph from one flowing shape into another; or the majestic sight and void filling sound of thousands of pink-footed geese rising with the dawn's light to herald the day.

It wouldn't do for all these bird species to compete for the same food source, so they evolved alongside each other to exploit different feeding niches. Those with large eyes and short beaks, such as the plovers, feed by sight, picking prey items from the surface. Those with longer beaks, such as redshanks and bar-tailed godwits, are able to probe deeper into the soft mud and locate their prey by touch. The long curved beak of the curlew is ideal for extracting deeper lying lugworms and ragworms from their burrows. Oystercatchers either hammer their way into a shell or prise apart the two halves of a bivalve to extract the animal within. Wigeon and brent geese graze the *Enteromorpha* and eel grass beds. Little egrets stalk the pools and shallows and creeks for fish.

As the tide advances, putting a lid on the estuary feeding ground, the saltmarsh can become a favoured roost site, allowing birds the chance to sleep and preen. The seed rich, salt tolerant plants of the marsh also cater for a number of feeding birds, particularly dabbling ducks such as teal, but also small passerines such as finches, larks and buntings. These in turn may be a target for a wintering merlin or hen harrier. The short vegetation is grazed by geese as well as by rabbits or voles and short-eared owls have a particular liking for the latter!

A winter's day on the estuary and marsh entrances and enchants like no other.

Donna Nook

The brownest November day imaginable. Brown mud, brown marsh, brown seals, brown sea. Even the sky was brown. But this maternity area for up to 1,100 grey seals is such a life affirming sight that any brownness is immaterial. Besides, the cream-pale newly born pups provide contrasting focal points to the scene. This thick, furry coat, or lanugo, is retained for two or three weeks whilst the single pup is dependent on its mother. Her milk is as much as 60% fat (human milk in comparison is 3.5% fat) and in that time the weight of the pup will treble, whilst that of the female, or cow, may decrease by a third.

At the end of this lactation period the pups are abandoned to fend for themselves, though 40% of them do not survive their first year. The cows are then sexually receptive and the waiting males, or bulls, are more than ready, having fought or threatened each other, to establish territories or harems. A bull grey seal can weigh as much as 300 kg and witnessing a fight between two equally sized males is a fearsome experience.

There was much sedentary behaviour on my visit, despite the odd testosterone laden skirmish, although the variety and volume of sounds would have suggested otherwise. Heard from some distance away, there was a range of assorted grunts, snorts, wails, barks, retches and the mightily impressive blubbery belly slaps of the bulls. The latter is a demonstration of their size and strength. They were not kidding!

The best time to visit Donna Nook for the seals is from early November to mid December. The mud and saltmarsh area is backed by a narrow belt of sand dunes, with thickets of buckthorn attractive to migrant birds and autumn thrushes, such as fieldfares and redwings.

Cow and Pup

Grey Seals,
Donna Nook, Lincolnshire.
Oil

132 ESTUARIES AND SALTMARSH

Bull Grey Seal

Donna Nook, Lincolnshire.
Oil

Coming Through

The very brownness of the day posed a challenge back in the studio when it came to creating a piece that was visually interesting. The elements of this composition were promising in themselves. The alertness of the foreground seals and the flying birds passing through created a swirling movement around the snoozing bull. Do I reproduce the colours, which may be accurate and authentic to that moment, but would produce a dull painting?

So I exaggerated what directional light there was, introduced strong warm and cold colours that played off each other, employed some vigorous mark making, and was altogether happier with the result as a painting in its own right.

This approach is often more satisfying creatively, when it works, forcing me to think and act as an artist rather than concerned with documenting a specific moment in time.

Lapwing and grey seals,
Donna Nook, Lincolnshire
Mixed Media

DRAWN TO THE EDGE   135

The Other Way Up
The test of this drawing is whether or not it works when you turn it upside down   The seals seemed utterly relaxed whichever way up they were   In a very large bean bag sort of way

Grey Seals,
Donna Nook, Lincolnshire.
Watercolour and pencil

Blakeney
Norfolk.
Watercolour

ESTUARIES AND SALTMARSH

Sand Martins
Early spring migrants that nest colonially in inland sand banks   These birds were hawking an autumn leaning saltmarsh   One last feed before departing south

Sand Martins,
Garlieston, Dumfries and Galloway
Acrylic and pastel

140   ESTUARIES AND SALTMARSH

Noble Curlew
A rare painting in gouache for me

Rough Firth
Dumfries and Galloway
Gouache

Resting Oystercatchers
I know that at any moment they may well be off   but
while they rest peacefully   mercifully quiet   twisting
occasionally   weathervaned in the breeze   I can relax
and make a careful study of form and light

Rough Firth,
Dumfries and Galloway.
Mixed Media

Wild Sky
It is one of the reasons why I came here to live   Huge wild skies with winter integrated geese   Cannot be ignored

Carsethorn,
Dumfries and Galloway.
Oil

Drumburn Winter

This small piece was painted on location   Looking at it again   back in the studio   it just didn't convey how cold a day it had been   how numbingly cold I had become sitting there   Added more and more icy blues   if only to convince myself

Drumburn,
Dumfries and Galloway.
Oil

Morston Quay
Painted from within the car on an unimpressively damp grey day   Were these the colours that I was seeing   or   were these the colours that I wanted to see?

Morston,
Norfolk.
Watercolour and pencil

Bar-tailed godwits
The advantage of a longer beak is being able to feed even when the mud is covered   at least for a while

Rockcliffe,
Dumfries and Galloway.
Acrylic

Common Gulls
Pencil

Up to 50 short-eared owls and 30 long-eared owls had been observed coming in off the North Sea throughout this grey windswept November day   As the light faded this individual just made it over the shingle sea wall and now sat exhausted in the middle of the marsh   partly sheltered behind some tall vegetation   its head turning this way and that apprehensive   the short tufts on the top of its head raised in alarm

I had to crouch low behind a bush myself to find some respite from the wind in order to attempt some drawings   The longer it remained there the more concerned I became for its well being   As the emptying day neared its end I willed the bird to fly   but my lasting view of it was still the same   Spent a long time pondering its fate   Still do

Short Eared Owls
Cley.
Pencil and watercolour

Lapwing Colours
An irresistible varicoloured multi faceted sort of a bird
Especially when caught by the sun

Kilspindie,
East Lothian.
Oil

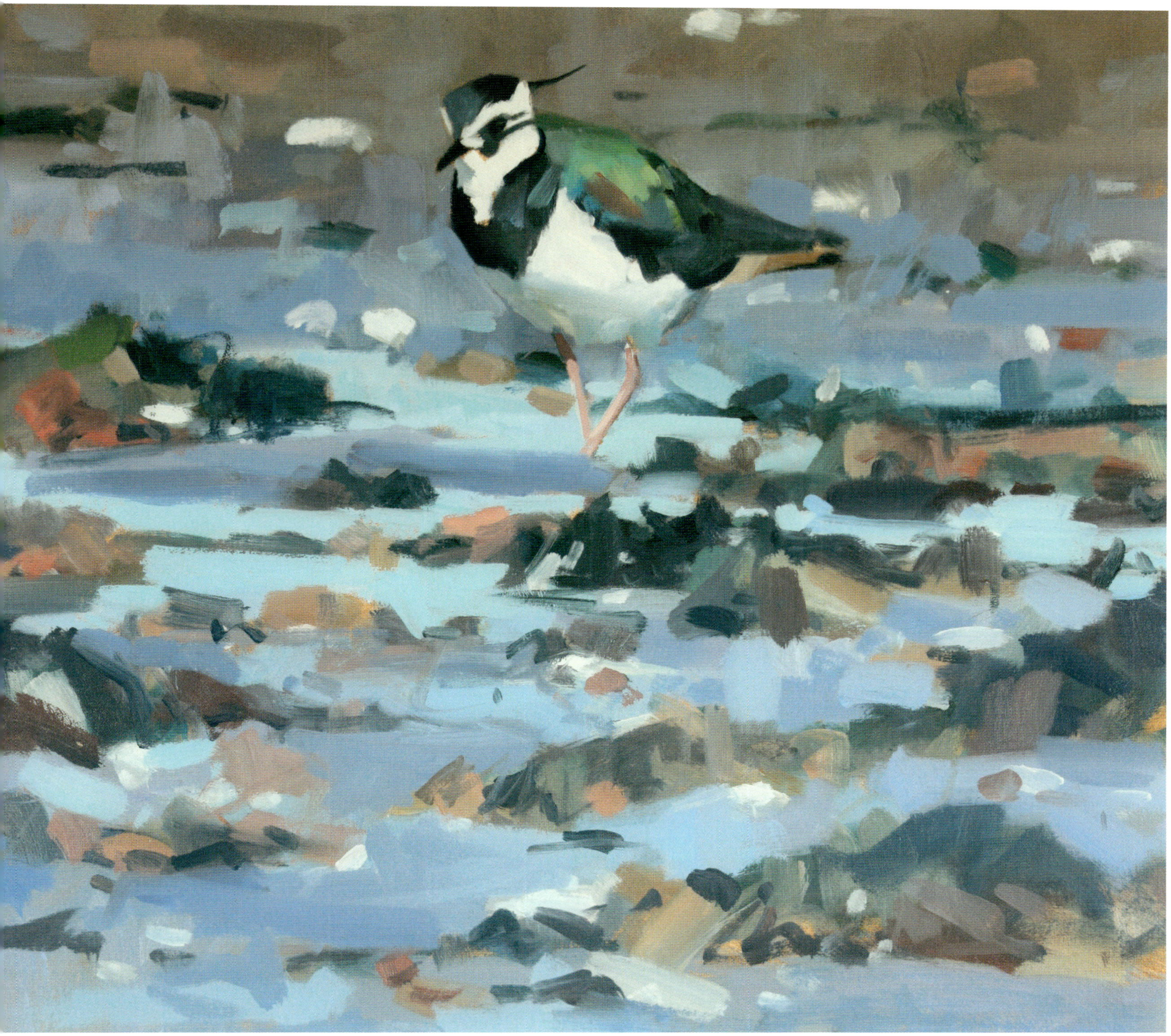

150 ESTUARIES AND SALTMARSH

Gilded Marsh

A litmus pink sky   Smouldering embers of marsh
Windless russets and golds   A gilded hand   Egrets
glowing like white paper lanterns   A female marsh
harrier balancing on a distant breeze   A suffocating
shadow rises to meet the horizon pulling skeins of geese
from the land to their roost   Snuffed out colours
Left to contemplate the purpling sky   And the quiet

Little Egret,
Stiffkey Marsh, North Norfolk.
Oil

Curlew Time
Despite the fact that the tide was low and feeding opportunities maximised these three curlews were in no rush   Down time matters to hand

Foulney Island,
Cumbria.
Acrylic

DRAWN TO THE EDGE

Spotted redshank
Morston Quay, Norfolk.
Pencil

Tollesbury Marsh
Deep cut channelled marsh   Arteries of opportunities
for feeding birds

Little Egret, Tollesbury, Essex.
Pastel

Dusk Arrivals
Family groups or larger skeins of barnacle geese entering their wintering refuge of Loch Gruinart at the end of a long days flight   The excited noise of 40,000 geese on the flats at the head of the loch the next evening was memorable   to say the least

Barnacle Geese,
Loch Gruinart, Islay.
Oil

Sea Lochs

Griburn,
Isle of Mull.
Pencil

The deeply fingered, fjord like lochs of Western Scotland can take the marine environment far inland. These seaweed fringed waters are the haunt of the otter and grey heron, but the sheltered nature of this habitat for winter storm plagued sea birds and mammals provides a welcome sanctuary. The seaweed also provides some nutritional value for the likes of red deer.

Sometimes it is just about the sitting. Camped on the banks of Loch Hourn, looking across sil-

Grey Heron
Gribun, Isle of Mull.
Pencil

vered waters to the full moon shadowed bulk of Beinn Sgritheall, it was no evening for sleeping inside. Huddled still, there was much satisfaction in just being; in the shallow, rippling wash of waves on the pebbled shore, a distant tree bound tawny owl, the lazy, deep winged darkened flight of a heron.

Movement close to my left; my eyes are the only thing to react. A female otter, out of the water, comes my way along the shoreline. She hesitates; something not quite right about this bit of coast this evening, strange new shapes, a sniff of something on the air. The waiting was entirely on her terms. Closer she came, silhouetted but for a lick of moonlight on whiskers and wet fur. Just ten feet away, investigating the shore in front of where I sat, breathless. She ambles on, my eyes following right until I can't see her without moving my head and I don't want to do that just yet. By the time I felt the moment had passed she was nowhere to be seen. Many minutes may have passed, I don't know.

Distant Cuillins
The Cuillins on Skye   Blue toothed on the horizon
Loch Carron narrowing far inland   Increasingly sheltered waters harbouring sea duck and divers   Bringing common seals to the heart of the Highlands   Otters abound

Loch Carron,
Plockton, Wester Ross.
Oil

The Otter's Wake
Lithe purposeful efficient playful   It always looks good fun being an otter   Free riding the fluidity and surging spontaneity of the sea

Kildonan,
Isle of Arran.
Acrylic on paper

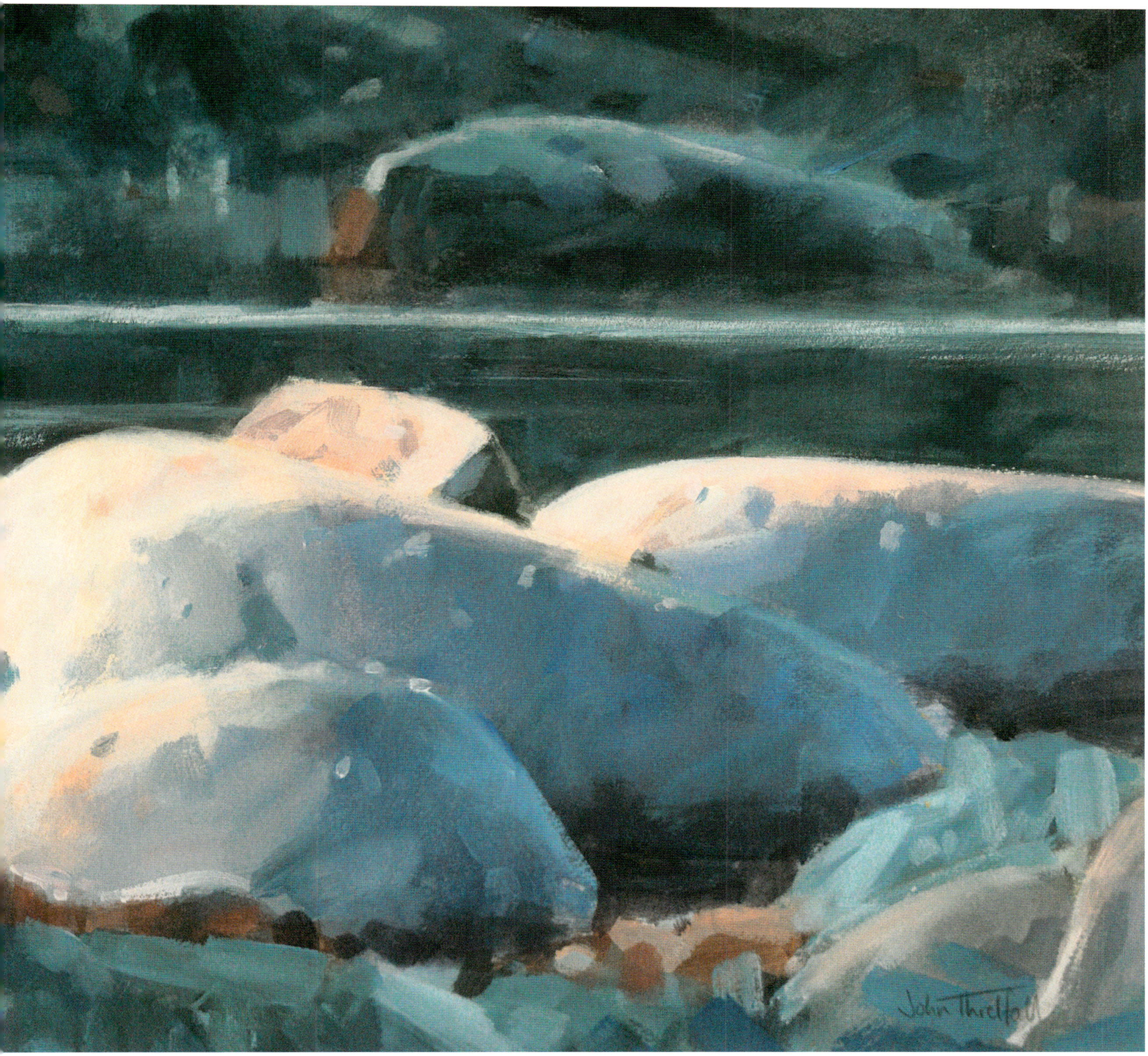
John Threlfall

Mute Swans with Scaup
Fresh water enters the salted loch   Attracts even sea
ducks and divers to bathe and drink

Bishop Burn, Loch Ryan,
Dumfries and Galloway.
Oil

White-tailed Eagle
Can a single bird transform a landscape as impressively as the white-tailed eagle?   The coast of Mull is wonderfully wild anyway   and then one of these comes along

Griburn,
Isle of Mull.
Oil

Arctic Terns,
Foulney Island.
Watercolour

OffShore Islands

As sea levels rose at the melting of the last Ice Age, and the land tilted as the weight of ice eased, many coastal areas were extensively flooded, isolating the British Isles from continental Europe and leaving only the higher ground showing as islands. The land is still tilting, very slowly. The smaller lumps of rock, of little use to ourselves, are now havens for seabirds, free from land predators such as foxes, stoats, rats and cats. A visit to one of these outposts, such as Skomer

Arctic Tern Display

Farne Islands, Northumberland.
Oil

Island off Pembrokeshire, or the Farne Islands off the Northumberland coast, is one of the most magical days out to be enjoyed in Britain.

The main seabird species may be the same as those on the mainland cliffs, but the absence of ground predators means that the level ground can be used as well as the vertical faces. Thus puffins can be found in much greater numbers and guillemots are able to populate the flat tops. Other species also feel safe enough to breed: arctic, common, Sandwich and roseate terns for example. Manx shearwaters, storm petrels and Leach's storm petrels all breed in internationally significant numbers on our coastal islands. Some waders, such as ringed plovers and oyster-catchers, nest here and arctic and great skuas can be found on the Northern Isles.

Eiders are among the many delights to be savoured on the Farne Islands. Known locally as Cuddy ducks, after Saint Cuthbert who lived on Inner Farne in the 6th century, the beautifully camouflaged females sit quietly on their nests alongside the paths or even under benches. It this approachability and tolerance by the majority of the birds that helps to make this trip an outstanding wildlife experience.

Arctic Terns
Foulney Island.
Watercolour

Then there are of course the gannet islands, Ailsa Craig, Boreray on St Kilda, Grassholm, the Bass Rock. These almost mythical sites comprise the greatest gannetries in the world. The Bass alone now holds 20% of the world's population. As many of our seabird populations decline, the numbers of gannets continue to grow. The gannet is supremely adapted to flying long distances in search of food, as is the fulmar, too, another recent success story. On soaring wings fulmars can travel far afield to feed on plankton or fish discards from trawlers, digesting the protein to leave a high energy concentrate in their stomachs that they can easily carry back to their hungry young.

These birds are at an advantage over the guillemot, for instance, which can only carry one fish at a time and has to make repeated short forays to the sea to feed its young. It partly resolves this problem by encouraging its young to take to the water after only three weeks, leading them to feeding grounds close by.

A day's excursion to the Farnes is not complete without a visit to the large grey seal colony and many of these small offshore islands are a first landfall and refuge for tired migrants. Anything may turn up, and a trip here, even well into the autumn, is well worth while.

Male Eiders and Arctic Terns,
Foulney Island, Cumbria
Watercolour

Arctic Tern,
Foulney Island.
Watercolour

168   OFF SHORE ISLANDS

That Way

Male Eiders,
Walney Island, Cumbria.
Oil

Parental Care

Kittiwakes, Farne Islands, Northumberland.
Mixed Media

DRAWN TO THE EDGE

Puffin Pair
The early summer weather of 2012 on the Farne Islands
was torrentially bad   Many many pufflings were
drowned in their burrows as they succumbed to flooding

Farne Islands,
Northumberland.
Acrylic on paper

Hestan Island
Midsummer's Day   Begun as a demonstration for a painting workshop to prompt dialogue and discussion and thoughts amongst the participants   Finished as a conversation between me   the canvas   and the tide

From Rockcliffe,
Dumfries and Galloway.
Mixed Media

Willow Warbler
The Carsaig coastline   Squeezed between the hard
edged sea and the high crafted cliffs   Free range goats
forage   Smell them before seeing them

South Walney,
Cumbria.
Oil

Gannet,
Bass Rock,
East Lothian.
Pencil

Wheatear
Walney Island.
Watercolour

The Bass Rock

The Bass Rock, just a half hour boat journey from North Berwick on the East Lothian coast, a dome shaped volcanic plug and for all the world looking as if it is besieged by snowfall whatever the degree of sunshine or cloud cover. Closer inspection reveals an effervescent seething of gannets, temporary home to 20% of the world's population. Over 50,000 pairs of Atlantic gannets are here to breed. That's a lot of birds!

It is one of the smelliest, noisiest, most fly infested places that I have ever visited. Once on the Rock, the path you walk up is inches deep in muddy guano and littered with decaying corpses of various vintages. It is however quite the most remarkable place I have ever visited. As I have heard said on a number of occasions 'forget the Maasai Mara, forget the Serengeti, here, just a few miles of the coast of the UK, is one of the great wildlife spectacles of the world'.

I was there with a group of artists to draw and paint but struggled to do either for a good long time. It is a sensationary overload on an incomprehensible scale. It is like being hit by a large wave, being knocked off balance, having the breath sucked out of you, not time after time but time without end, until you are back on the boat, halfway across to the mainland and the lustily gawking cacophony recedes, the birds thin out and the smell becomes only a memory…..or does it? With so many thousands of birds in the air above the Rock, hanging, landing and leaving in a tangled melee of flight lines, you are going to get splattered! Your clothes are going to bear witness to your visit for some time to come. To be honest, it was an honour to get crapped on by such an impressively gorgeous creature!

Make no mistake, the gannet is an impressively beautiful bird. Dazzlingly white, soft golden headed, powerful in flight, a black tipped cruciform against the sky, dramatically torpedo shaped as it dives from height into the sea to feed. Steadfastly loyal to both site and mate.

Where was I to start to portray this unruly stramash? Maybe I could start with one bird and work out from there? I sat down to draw, to focus on that piercing pale blue grey eye and the angles of the beak. As my concentration narrowed, the noise became more background than full frontal, the smell less odious and noticeable, the flies less irritating. I gave myself to that bird and to that drawing. For a few precious moments that is all there is……………..then WHAM! A very large, heavy, sharply pointed thing lands in my lap!! I don't know whos shock was the greater. The gannet slid to the ground and clambered away. I looked down at my bent drawing board and tried to regain some semblance of composure! With so little space available landing can be a tricky and undignified affair, running the gauntlet of daggered beaks and apologetic artists in their flight path.

The birds sit on a nest of seaweed and grass, more often than not incorporating brightly coloured nylon fishing lines and rope, a respectful-just-out-of-range-of-their-neighbours-beaks, length apart. Bickeringly noisy squabbles are frequent and in one such incident the egg of the bird that I was drawing became dislodged and rolled away. The bird didn't seem to notice and at the first available opportunity I returned the surprisingly small egg to its nest. The gannet settled down again as if nothing had happened.

It was an extraordinary privilege to spend time amongst these creatures, moving slowly and deferentially, feeling like the alien I undoubtedly was. It is not the squalid quarrelling that lingers but the absolute astonishment and awe at being present at the heart of this tumultuous spectacle.

Greetings

Gannets, Bass Rock,
East Lothian.
Oil

Duel

Gannets, Bass Rock,
East Lothian.
Pastel

Gannet, Bass Rock,
East Lothian.
Pencil

Gannets, Bass Rock,
East Lothian.
Watercolour

DRAWN TO THE EDGE

Don't Mess With Me
Nesting alongside the path   Much aggrieved whenever anybody walked past   No visit to the coast is complete without the indignant cries of the herring gull   Took a quick photo and left them to it

Herring Gull,
Bass Rock, East Lothian.
Oil

Bass Tumult

Gannets,
Bass Rock, East Lothian.
Watercolour and gouache

Gannet, Bass Rock,
East Lothian.
Watercolour

Sitting Tight
Since it last nested here this bird will have flown to the Antarctic and back   The Arctic tern sees more daylight than any other species on the planet   Awe and wonder is due

Arctic Tern, Farne Islands
Northumberland.
Mixed Media

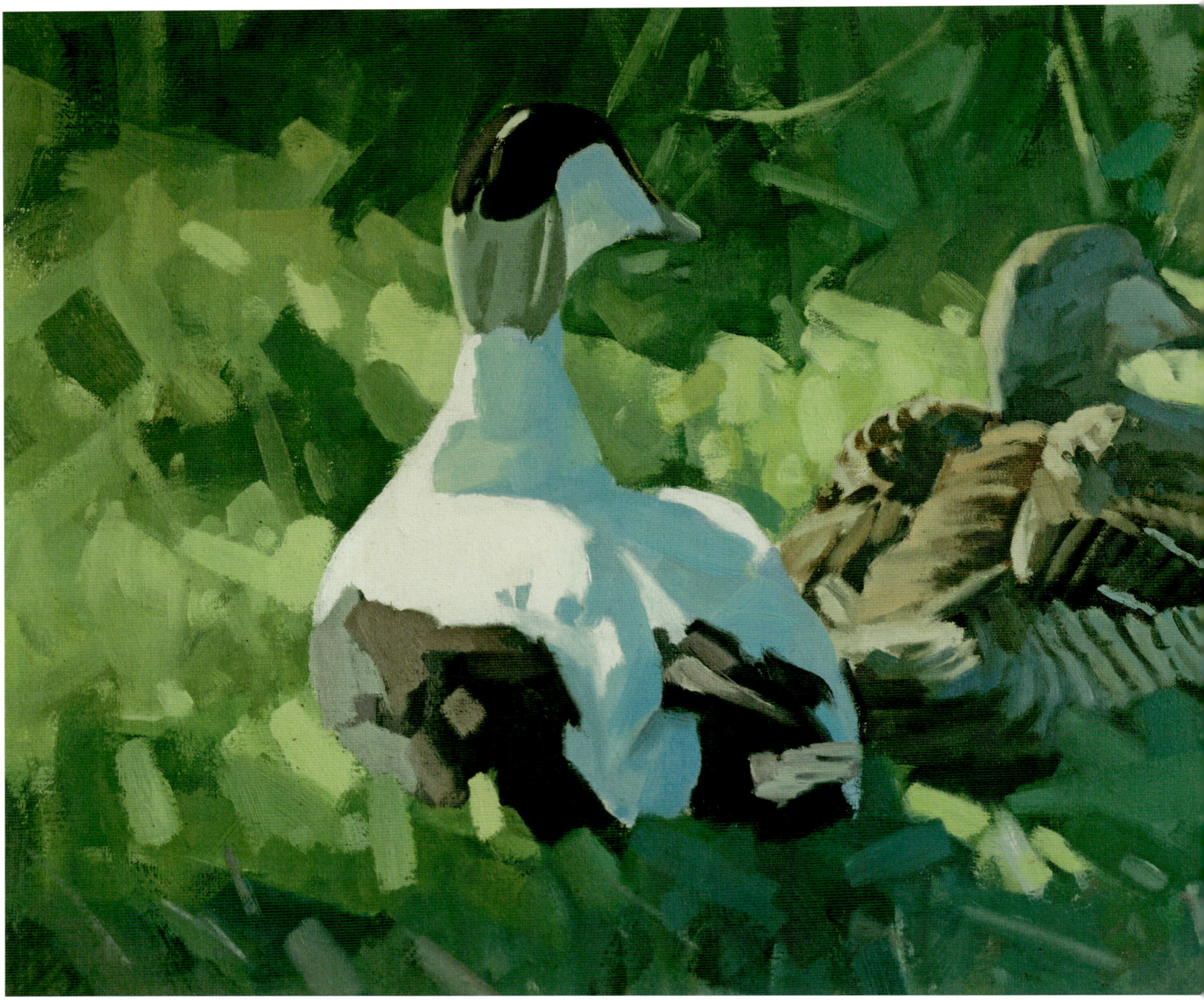

Eider Pair
Walney Island on the south west extremity of Cumbria has the southernmost breeding population of eiders in the UK

Walney Island,
Cumbria.
Oil

186   OFF SHORE ISLANDS

The Line Up

Guillemots,
Farne Islands,
Northumberland.
Mixed Media

Conclusion

The breathtaking array and wealth of wildlife around our shores enriches our lives beyond measure. Economically, nature based tourism provides jobs and a significant income for local communities. But the most important benefits are maybe less tangible: the exhilaration of watching diving gannets; witnessing at first hand the precarious existence of a young guillemot or the fragility of a newly hatched ringed plover chick; seeing an otter, any time, anywhere; joyously taking a short boat trip out to a seal colony: triumphantly finding a crab in a rock pool; being entranced by the elegance of arctic terns in flight ; delighting in the smile inducing, suggestive cooing of male eiders; being mesmerised by the thronging multitude of creatures at a big seabird colony. The list goes on. These are life affirming moments to be relished and celebrated. To be thrilled, amazed, in awe of the planetary wonders that the UK coast bestows upon us elevates our days, pitches them to a level way above the ordinary or mundane.

A number of years ago, my father and I took an ageing family friend to Bempton Cliffs in East Yorkshire. Margaret had collected puffin images and sculptures and souvenirs for many years but had never seen the "real" thing. We were hoping to rectify that situation. Sure enough, Bempton duly obliged, and I positioned the telescope so that she could look through it and at the puffin. She stood there transfixed until the tears were rolling down her cheeks. Puffins can do that to you.

To read of these riches is to think that everything is fine and rosy with this part of our natural heritage. To be out there seeing it for yourself is to realise that something is not quite right with our coastal and marine environment. Some of our sea cliffs are quieter than they used to be. This is particularly so in the Northern Isles of Orkney and Shetland. In the last 30 years, kittiwakes and guillemots have declined here by 90%. Guillemots, razorbills and puffins are almost entirely reliant on a single food source, sand eels, and there is no doubt that these vital, protein rich fish are in short supply. A warming of the sea has affected the plankton on which the sand eels feed. A recent report in Scottish Birds, published by the Scottish Ornithologists' Club, illustrates the rate of warming, by citing the movement north of the 10*C isotherm in the North Sea at "c.22 km per year over the last 50 years'". That is an incredibly sobering statistic.

There is no doubt also that intensively trawled and fished seas are going to have a major impact on the availability of food for seabirds and marine mammals. Sand eels, being rich in oil, have even been used as fuel for Danish power stations. Discards from trawlers have however benefited some seabirds such as gannets and fulmars. These are birds able to travel long distances from their breeding colonies to find food.

New knowledge is required to discover where the best feeding grounds for seabirds are located and indeed GPS technology is being used to monitor the daily movements of some birds. Kittiwakes and guillemots are having to fly further and further to find food and then are only able to bring back one fish at a time. Our major land based breeding colonies have designated protection, but binding marine protection legislation is much needed and still not in place.

The brightly coloured, discarded, synthetic netting from the fishing industry finds its way into the nests of some larger birds, such as gannets, cormorants and shags. Here the young birds may become entangled and, unable to free themselves, they will die. A fulmar on the Farne Islands was seen to cough up a lump of plastic. Even the shorelines of remote Hebridean beaches are not safe from the scourge of man's "disposable" lifestyle. It is now reported that every single handful of sand you grasp on any UK beach will contain plastic, however small.

Only concerted efforts to eradicate introduced species, such as rats and mink, from some islands has saved seabird colonies there. Birds nesting in burrows, such as shearwaters, have been especially vulnerable.

Chemical pollutants that end up in the marine food chain, and oil spills, will take their toll. Many of our seabirds spend the entire winter at sea and are vulnerable to these hazards. Severe winter storms may also adversely affect populations and the advent of offshore renewable energy schemes is another problem yet to be evaluated.

Despite this liturgy of predicaments it has to be said that seabirds are extremely hardy souls. Many of the species can live 40 years or more, and, if time allows, can also be adaptable. Thereby may lie the biggest problem of all. The rate of change to the environment on which they depend is so rapid that they may not have that time. It is our moral and ethical duty to ensure that they do.